"At the moment, what passes for political debate is the bickering of two vociferous and wrong-headed parties. Robert Jensen reacquaints us with the political and social skills we'll need if we're to reclaim politics for the 21st century. This is a brave book, one that packs more wisdom in its few pages than a shelf's worth of political theory, because it's also a book about political practice. Jensen patiently, honestly, and rigorously exemplifies the highest virtues of a public intellectual." —Raj Patel, author of *Stuffed and Starved: Markets, Power and the Hidden Battle for the World's Food System*

"The first date or dinner party taboo is famous: 'No religion, no politics.' Debating, discussion, engagement with ideas that matter—these are all supposed to be left to professionals, specialists who talk to each other in mutually incomprehensible ways. Meanwhile decades of advertising, sound bites, PR, filtered information, and internet trolling have numbed us even more. But we don't have to live this way. We could immediately start living in a better world, one in which every conversation was an opportunity to learn more about ourselves, others, and the precious little world we all have to try to live on together. To do that, though, we would have to re-learn how to think and talk, how to agree and disagree. Robert Jensen's *Arguing For Our Lives* can help us do that." —Justin Podur, author of *Haiti's New Dictatorship*

"*Arguing for Our Lives* is a crucial book for reclaiming not only the pedagogical and political virtues of critical thinking, but for securing the foundations for critical agency and engaged citizenship. This is an indispensable book for students, educators, and others willing to fight the current ongoing assault by religious, political, and moral fundamentalists on critical thought, if not reason itself, that has engulfed American politics. Everyone should read *Arguing for Our Lives* if they believe there is a connection between how we think and how we act, how we understand democracy and how we experience and struggle for it." —Henry Giroux, author of *Twilight of the Social: Resurgent Politics in the Age of Disposability and Disposable Youth*

Arguing for Our Lives

Arguing for Our Lives

A User's Guide to Constructive Dialog

Robert Jensen

City Lights Books | San Francisco

Cover design: MILLER 360

Introductory quote by James Baldwin is from his essay "As Much Truth As One Can Bear," in Randall Kenan, ed., *The Cross of Redemption: Uncollected Writings* (New York: Pantheon, 2010), p. 34.

Library of Congress Cataloging-in-Publication Data
Jensen, Robert, 1958 July 14–
  Arguing for our lives : a user's guide to constructive dialog / Robert Jensen.
    pages cm
  ISBN 978-0-87286-573-0
1. Reasoning. 2. Thought and thinking. I. Title.

BC177.J46 2013
160—dc23

2012049282

E-edition also available: 978-0-87286-605-8

City Lights Books are published at the City Lights Bookstore
261 Columbus Avenue, San Francisco, CA 94133
www.citylights.com

"Not everything that is faced can be changed; but nothing can be changed until it is faced."
—James Baldwin

Contents

The Age of Anxiety

It would be tempting to say that we live today in *the* Age of Anxiety, if such an age hadn't already been proclaimed in the last century, first in Europe after World War I and then across the whole world in the nuclear age. Poet W.H. Auden won the 1948 Pulitzer Prize for his book *The Age of Anxiety: A Baroque Eclogue*, which struggled—mostly unsuccessfully—with the search for hope in a modern industrial world drained of meaning:

> Both professor and prophet depress,
> For vision and longer view
> Agree in predicting a day
> Of convulsion and vast evil . . .

Auden didn't express a lot of confidence in his fellow citizens' abilities to change course:

> We would rather be ruined than changed,
> We would rather die in our dread
> Than climb the cross of the moment
> And let our illusions die.[1]

While the number of prescriptions that doctors in the United States today write for anxiety disorders might suggest our own moment in history is particularly anxious,[2] we should step back and think of all of recorded human history as an anxious age. Ever since we humans created what we call "civilization" and started the project of living beyond the planet's means and beyond our own capabilities, it has been inevitable that human societies would struggle with anxiety. The further we overreach—creating complex societies too big to manage, drawing down the ecological capital of Earth—the more intense the collective anxiety. Our problem is not just the many anxious individuals who have particular trouble coping, but ways of living that aren't designed for the type of animals that we are, as we try to micro-manage a world that is too vast and complex for us to control. Our collective anxiety is not an aberration but a predictable outcome of a simple truth:

> For ten millennia, we have been a species out of context.[3]

Let's put the anxiety of our age in this larger historical framework. The genus *Homo* goes back a couple of million years, and our species, *Homo sapiens*, has been around for about 200,000 years. What we call civilization, which arose with the invention of agriculture, starts only about 10,000 years ago. What today we take to be normal ways of organizing human societies are, in fact, recent developments, radically different from the way we lived for 95 percent of our evolutionary history. We evolved in small gatherer-hunter groups, band-level societies that were probably well under one hundred members and organized internally in much more egalitarian fashion than the way we live today.[4] Research on human social networks suggest that there is a limit on the "natural" size of a human social group of about 150 members, which is determined by our cognitive capacity. This has been called "Dunbar's number," after anthropologist Robin Dunbar: the number of individuals with whom any one of us can maintain stable relationships.[5]

When we create social, political, and economic systems that require us to deal with more people and more complex relationships in hierarchies, we are living outside of our evolutionary context. When individual humans are taken out of familiar settings and plopped down in brand-new places, we get a bit anxious. What is true for us as individuals is true at this larger level. Life out of context is bound to be an anxious life.

This out-of-context existence produces a baseline anxiety, from which we see spikes at particular moments in history when we humans seemed incapable of managing ourselves in any sort of rational and humane manner. In the twentieth century, we saw that happen after the mass slaughter of World War I, when the best and the brightest of Europe had just finished fighting a war that reached new levels of barbarism. After World War II, during which the barbarism returned in full force, humans were left to ponder the possiblitiy of complete annihilation in the nuclear age.

There is plenty of horror in the world today—both in the intense, sporadic violence of war and in the ongoing, everyday suffering that results from global inequality—but humans also have taken some steps forward in our dealings with each other. In relations within and between societies, there has been progress, albeit fitful and uneven. Slavery is illegal and has been abolished in practice in most places. In many societies there is recognition of the value of cultural diversity. Gender and racial equality have advanced in significant ways. There is much work to be done to produce a more just world, but one can see the path for moving forward.

But there is a good reason we may be in a distinctive age of anxiety, if we take seriously the more intractable problems on the ecological front, where the news is bad beyond the telling. Consider this warning from 1,700 of the world's leading scientists:

> Human beings and the natural world are on a collision course. Human activities inflict harsh and often irreversible damage on the environment and on critical resources. If not checked, many of our current practices put at serious risk the future that we wish for human society and the plant and animal kingdoms, and may so alter the living world that it will be unable to sustain life in the manner that we know. Fundamental changes are urgent if we are to avoid the collision our present course will bring about.[6]

That statement was issued in 1992, and in the subsequent two decades humans made no significant course corrections. For anyone looking at the data on our multiple, cascading ecological crises; for anyone thinking about the trajectory of human life on the planet; for anyone who feels a connection to what is dying all around us—the severity of the human attack on the living world can produce intense anxiety. Our age of anxiety today is rooted in these unfolding ecological disasters and a growing realization that we have disrupted natural forces in ways we do not understand and cannot control. As Bill McKibben puts it, "The world hasn't ended, but the world as we know it has—even if we don't quite know it yet."[7]

McKibben, the first popular writer to alert the world to the threat of climate change, argues that humans have so dramatically changed the planet's ecosystems that we should rename the Earth, call it Eaarth:

> The planet on which our civilization evolved no longer exists. The stability that produced that civilization has vanished; epic changes have begun. We may, with commitment and luck, yet be able to maintain a planet that will sustain some kind of civilization, but it won't be the same planet, and hence it won't be the same civilization. The earth that we knew—the only earth that we ever knew—is gone.[8]

If McKibben is accurate—and I think the evidence supports his assessment—then some level of anxiety would be an appropriate reaction to our situation. We can't pretend that all we need to do is tinker with existing systems to fix a few environmental problems. Massive changes in how we live are required, what McKibben characterizes as a new kind of civilization. No matter where any one of us fits in the social and economic hierarchies, there is no escape from the dislocations of such changes. Money and power might insulate some people from the most wrenching consequences of these shifts, but there is no escape. That long-standing anxiety produced by living out of our evolutionary context is intensified to unprecedented levels by ecological crises that force us to recognize that we do not live in stable societies and no longer live on a stable planet. We may feel safe and secure in specific places at specific times, but it's hard to believe in any safety and security in a collective sense.

This is not the preface to a naïve argument that we return to gathering and hunting; with 7 billion people on the planet, obviously we couldn't go back even if we wanted to. Just as naïve would be to believe we can count on human ingenuity and "advanced" technology to save the day. There is no magic to be conjured that can re-create an idyllic past or create a utopian future.

Instead, we need to start facing the sources of our anxiety so that we can honestly face reality and develop better coping strategies. Right now, the most affluent and technologically sophisticated society in the history of the world—the United States—seems more committed to deep denial than to enlightened engagement with this anxiety. A good first step in that engagement would be recognizing that our anxiety is a product of our arrogance; that the cure for that arrogance is recognition of our ignorance; and that understanding our ignorance—the limits of human intelligence—will help us, paradoxically, develop the critical intellectual skills we need to face the challenges ahead.

Arrogance

Just as we typically think of anxiety as a characteristic of individuals, so do we speak of arrogance in individual terms. We all know people who are haughty and unjustifiably overconfident, and we recognize that we all have within ourselves that weakness. But the focus here is the collective arrogance of the modern human. Since the invention of agriculture, we humans have used our well-developed cognitive capacities to control our environments and manipulate other species to our advantage, and that success has led to arrogance. The development of modern science put that arrogance on steroids, as humans began to believe we could—almost literally—run the world as if we were gods.

That arrogance is what has transformed Earth into Eaarth. We can intervene to bend natural systems to our will, but we lack the capacity to control the consequences of our intervention. We are really, really smart, but we have not been quite smart enough to see the limits of our intelligence.

Facing that fact, we have two choices. One is to believe that we will find solutions to all our problems through more sophisticated technology. This is what some of us have begun to call "technological fundamentalism," which today takes the form of a quasi-religious belief that the use of advanced technology is always a good thing and that any problems caused by the unintended consequences of such technology can be remedied by more technology. Finding themselves in a hole that they have dug, technological fundamentalists argue for digging deeper and more furiously. In 1968, Stewart Brand began the *Whole Earth Catalog* with that famous line, "We are as gods and might as well get used to it."[9] Four decades later, Brand wrote that this suggestion had become an imperative: "We are as gods and HAVE to get good at it."[10] For some, the solution lies in intensifying our commitment to the delusion that got us into the mess in the first place.

The other choice is to recognize that we are fundamentally ignorant in the face of a world whose complexity we not only can't control but can't begin to adequately describe.

Given the success of science in revealing physical processes heretofore unknown to us, the appropriate response should be not arrogance but the recognition of human limits. The more we know, the more we should be aware of what we don't know, and likely will never know.

This is not a suggestion that we celebrate stupidity, nor is it an atavistic call for abandoning science. Rather, we would be wise to adopt what plant geneticist Wes Jackson calls "an ignorance-based worldview": whatever our technical and scientific prowess, we are—and always will be—far more ignorant than knowledgeable.[11] Acknowledging our basic ignorance does not mean we should revel in the ways humans can be dumb, but rather that we should recognize our obligation to act as intelligently as possible, keeping in mind not only what we know but how much we don't know.[12]

Again, to be clear: Nothing in this view argues for abandoning all hope of knowing anything, for giving up on the search for truth, or for concluding in despair that we can discover nothing upon which we can act with confidence. It is not a plea to renounce science or to seek answers purely on nonrational grounds, but is simply a call for intellectual humility.

An obvious example: Technological fundamentalists are comfortable with pursuing nuclear energy, despite the potentially catastrophic consequences of a reactor accident and even though there remains no workable system of safely disposing of the waste. Folks endorsing an ignorance-based worldview would counsel against the development of an energy-production process that presents those risks and depends on the promise of some future solution to the waste problem.

If, as Jackson suggests, we were to understand that "knowledge is not adequate to run the world," then before embarking on a scientific or technological venture we would ask, "How many people will be involved? At what level of culture? Will we be able to back out? Scientists, technologists, and policy-makers would be assiduous students of exits." If we had taken those questions seriously, we would not have embarked on the disastrous nuclear project.

Adopting an ignorance-based world view doesn't mean we should ignore our intellectual capacities; in fact, it demands more of each one of us. When we recognize that experts can't answer all our questions, and that sometimes experts' hubris can get us in trouble, then sharpening our critical thinking skills becomes more important than ever. An ignorance-based worldview is a call to that critical thinking.

CHAPTER 1

In Defense of Intellectual Life

There are two clichés about our intellectual lives that illustrate contemporary U.S. culture's confusion and cowardice. One is the response to one's attempt to analyze a difficult problem: "You think too much." The second is the common advice for getting along in groups: "Don't talk about religion or politics."

On the first cliché: Yes, it's possible to overthink, if we engage in endless analyzing as a way to avoid taking action we should take, or if we get stuck in our heads and cut ourselves off from our experience and emotions. We don't want to fall into passivity or disembodied abstraction. But too often in this culture, when we want to tackle a tough problem and think it through carefully, we will be accused of thinking too much, as if somehow the problems we face can, and should, be handled without using our intellect.

On the second cliché: If we don't talk about religion or politics, what else is there of interest to discuss? In this context, I'm defining "religion" broadly, as wrestling with ultimate questions of existence that are wrapped up in the query "What does it mean to be a human being?" I'm using "politics" broadly as well, to mean the quest to answer the unavoidable question in any society, "How should power and resources be distributed?"

We all should think a lot, especially about religion and politics. We should all be striving to be the best critically thinking intellectuals we can be.

Both those terms—critical thinking and intellectual—come with some baggage. Some people fear that encouraging "critical thinking" is really a euphemism for an attack on traditional values, especially those rooted in religious faith. And many assume that "intellectuals" are elitist snobs who tout their academic credentials as proof of superiority. Both terms can be misused that way, of course, but that is not the only fate for critically thinking intellectuals.

Critical thinking should lead us to evaluate all claims, including "traditional values," and that means that individuals and societies will on occasion have to abandon some of those traditions. The world came to abandon the traditional values that justified slavery and defined women as the property of men, and most of us agree that was a good thing. But critical thinking can not only lead to challenges to tradition but can also help us understand the strength of some of those values. A critique of hierarchical male-dominated models of family, for example, can lead to greater appreciation for the way in which more egalitarian models of family can help connect people in healthy communities.

Critical thinking also should be applied to new ideas, to help us separate important insights from faddish claims. Such critical thinking applied, for example, to each new diet plan that promises to make losing unwanted weight easy would save people a lot of money and heartache. In the classroom, critical thinking applied to postmodern literary theory could save countless students from slogging through attempts to explain literature in arcane academic language and would likely increase their appreciation of literature.

Some kinds of intellectual work require specialized training, which means some people will play special roles in some endeavors. In a technologically advanced society, obviously no one person can acquire the knowledge of every technology; we will have to rely on specialists' expertise in some arenas. But especially on matters of social, political, and economic policy, everyone is capable of developing the intellectual abilities needed to contribute to the cultural conversation about our goals. We don't need to be specialists to develop viewpoints we can defend in dialog with others. In a healthy democratic system, experts serve the greater good rather than dictate it.

To create a culture in which people aspire to be critically thinking intellectuals, we must overcome the negative connotations of the terms. That effort would be aided immensely if those people who are paid to do intellectual work—professors, teachers, clergy, journalists, and writers—were to demystify their work. I have been a university professor for more than two decades, and the longer I teach, the more I talk with students about the process by which I come to understand a concept or answer a question. My goal is not to showcase my allegedly superior intellect but to demonstrate how we all can work our way through a problem. That's not false modesty; I believe I have something important to offer the students as a result of my intellectual work, but I don't believe that I have some special gift that gives me an advantage. Whatever I know is the result of effort and struggle, not genius. My job is to make that process attractive and attainable, not shroud my professional status in a mystical aura.

Even with these attempts at the demystification of intellectual life, in my experience many students are nervous about applying critical thinking and most are reluctant to identify as intellectuals. For some time, I've been tempted to ask my students, in jest, "Are you now, or have you ever been, an intellectual?" One semester, I finally did that.

In my introductory journalism class at the University of Texas at Austin, I told students at I was going to take a risk and ask some of them to come out in front of their classmates. I feigned nervousness and warned them that I wasn't sure if this was a wise thing to do, but that I needed to know more about them for the next section of the course. Instead of asking if any of the students were gay or lesbian—the identities typically associated with coming out—I posed a different question: How many of you, I asked, are intellectuals? How many, I asked, are willing to stand up in front of others and publicly declare, "I am an intellectual!"

The students chuckled, then looked nervously at each other when they realized I was serious. No one stood at first. I repeated the question: "There are two hundred of you in this room, all college students attending a prestigious institution of higher learning, and not one of you is an intellectual?" Finally one student stood and then a few others, but no more than a dozen were willing to claim the label.

After the exercise, we talked about why university students, no matter what their academic major or particular interests, might reject the label "intellectual." As I expected, some associated the term with elitism, a claim that one is smarter than everyone else. Others assumed it is a term that describes certain professional positions, such as university professors, and it would be dishonest to embrace the identity themselves. Some likely refused because by that point, late in the semester, they were skeptical of identifying with anything I suggested.

I told them that as journalists, or prospective journalists, their hesitation wasn't surprising to me. Most working journalists would reject the term, mostly to avoid being seen as snobby. But I pressed them to consider how we could use the term in a positive fashion, not just as a label for certain professions and not as an assertion of arrogance.

What would it mean to be serious about being a critically thinking intellectual? First, the term "intellectual work" is not just a synonym for "thinking." Every day, everyone thinks about things. Intellectual work suggests a systematic effort to (1) collect relevant information, (2) analyze that information to discern patterns that help deepen our understanding of how the world works, and (3) use that understanding to make judgments about how to try to shape our world. The key is "systematic effort," which requires intention and discipline. We all think, but intellectual work means organized thinking to reach conclusions for a purpose. When it's defined that way, it becomes clear that lots of different kinds of people do intellectual work—not just writers and professors, but students, organizers, political activists, researchers of various kinds. They engage in that systematic effort in search of the answers to questions about the natural world, technology, human behavior, societies. Some focus on fairly small questions while others look more broadly.

We should add three important qualifications to this defense of intellectual work.

First, this definition of intellectual work doesn't assume

a simplistic dichotomy between work done with our minds and work done with our bodies. All the work we do in the world involves some combination of our minds and bodies. Anyone with experience in the skilled trades, such as plumbing or carpentry, knows that work requires not just physical exertion but a sharp mind that can assess a problem and plan the appropriate steps to complete a task. Successful gardening requires a lot of digging, weeding, and hauling, but also involves an extraordinary amount of knowledge about the way that air, water, soil, plants, and animals interact. Even basic manual labor requires thought about how to perform a task efficiently. I once had a warehouse job that involved unloading trucks and stacking boxes of building supplies, and what I remember about it is not just the physical labor but the craft of coordinating the unloading with other workers and constructing the stacks of boxes in a stable fashion—the more careful the construction of the stack, the higher we could stack the boxes without them falling. In that case, the intellectual work was relatively simple and solved a problem of limited interest to others, but it demonstrates the capacity we all have to be systematic in our thinking.

Second, not all intellectual work involves critical thinking. Many jobs in the so-called "information economy" involve exercising the intellect but require no critical thinking in the way I am using the term. Some of that work is clerical in nature, shifting data from one place to another or one form to another, with little serious reflection needed by a worker. One can open an academic journal and read articles in which the author demonstrates an understanding of various theories and methods, presenting information but employing little rigorous self-reflection and limited critical thinking.

Third, what the culture labels intellectual work is not more important than, or superior to, other categories of work. It's obvious that those people who are paid to do work that is primarily intellectual wouldn't last long if others weren't engaged in work that creates food, shelter, clothing, and other necessities. When a society is affluent enough to subsidize intellectuals, often those given the privilege of doing intellectual work create the illusion of their greater value, which we should reject.

We shouldn't assume that only those being employed in primarily intellectual vocations have the capacity or the duty to be thinking critically. In a healthy society, everyone would understand themselves as intellectuals. In a healthy democracy, all citizens would see intellectual work as part of their political obligation.

CHAPTER 2

Intellectual Basics:
Simple but Not Simplistic

To make the case that everyone is capable of critical thinking is not to suggest that all contributions from everyone have equal standing or that there are no guidelines for good intellectual practice. We all should weigh in on questions, but our contributions should be scrutinized according to agreed-upon standards. In this chapter I offer not a detailed technical approach to critical thinking, but rather a series of framing questions that can help us tackle the important issues we face in the realms of social, economic, and political policy.

Let's start with suggestions for examining the claims we all make. As we engage intellectually to deepen our understanding of the world—whether it be the physical world of which we humans are a part, or the social world that we humans create—we should always be asking four basic questions about a claim being made:

- What are the unstated assumptions behind the
  claim, and how do those assumptions affect our
  understanding?

- How are terms being defined, and might those definitions favor one position over another?
- What is the quality of the evidence being offered, and is the full range of evidence being acknowledged?
- Does the evidence lead in logical fashion to the claim being made?

All arguments are not created equal. Upon examination, some will be stronger than others and some will be without merit. These four basic questions provide a starting point for that assessment, yet they are routinely ignored, not just in everyday argument but in mainstream political discourse. People are tempted to avoid that intellectual engagement, perhaps in part because they want to avoid the conflict that might follow, but also perhaps because intellectual work takes effort. The more complicated and confusing the world gets, the more seductive it is to believe that all claims are mere opinion. From that perspective, one isn't obligated to evaluate another's argument but can simply dismiss it as inconsistent with one's own beliefs. Reducing all arguments to the exchange of opinions is the lazy way out. That's why I stop students any time they begin a contribution in class with, "Well, this is just my opinion, but. . . ."

"What do you mean by 'just your opinion'?" I ask. "Did you pull this opinion out of thin air, or is it the product of some research and thinking? Can you defend your assumptions, define your terms clearly, offer evidence and reasoning to support your opinion? If you can, why undermine your argument by suggesting it is 'just your opinion,' which invites others not to take it seriously?"

I press these points because we live in a culture in which

the skills of intellectual and political engagement are atrophying. Too many people equate "argument" with the inane shouting matches between pundits on cable television talk shows, rather than with the careful defense of a position and a response to challenges. In a hyper-mediated culture awash with people pontificating, it's easy to abandon the work of assessing arguments—to give up on what seems like an endless task of evaluation—and shrug off opportunities for critical engagement with "Well, that's just your opinion."

Yes, everyone has opinions and we all have a right to our opinions. However, opinions are meaningful to the degree that we make it clear to others why we hold those opinions and give them good reasons to consider our ideas. All of life is not a formal debate, and students exploring their ideas in class shouldn't be expected to articulate a fully formed defense of every claim made. But in a healthy classroom students should be encouraged—even pressed—to sharpen, articulate, and defend their opinions. In a healthy democracy, the same can be said of citizens.

What will help us move forward in this goal? There are many books about argumentation and rhetoric, about formal and informal logic, about the fallacies that are used in constructing bad arguments.[1] The goal here is not to summarize those traditional approaches but instead to frame our critical thinking at this moment in history, as we face vexing problems in our attempts to create a more just and sustainable world. I begin with suggestions about how we should approach these questions, and then remind us of our limits before sketching a way to think about what we can achieve.

I want to start with the most basic of questions, one we all struggle with when young and which most of us never completely resolve: Who am I? Wrestling with that basic question of identity can easily turn self-indulgent and narcissistic, but it also can be a path to greater understanding not only of self but of the world. Let's think about the question at three levels:

- Ecological: On what principles should my relationship to the non-human world be grounded, and how does that relationship define me?
- Societal: On what principles should my relationships to others be grounded, and how do those relationships define me?
- Personal: What aspects of my unique personality are most central to who I am?

On the ecological: Asking about our relationship to the "non-human world" rather than to "nature" reminds us that we are part of nature, not separate from it. Nature, in this sense, is the whole living world, of which humans are one small, but significant, part. This change in terminology shifts our frame of reference and asks us to think about ourselves not as the center of the world, but as one component of it. How we define ourselves personally will depend in part on how we understand the human family in relation to that living world.

The same is clearly the case in societal terms; our sense of self is connected to how we understand our relationship to others. Just as we aren't beings who float above and apart from the world, we don't exist outside social groups. Before we ask "Who am I?" in the most personal sense—the focus on what makes us individual and unique—we should situate ourselves not only in society but in the living world. The personal question is important, but it is better understood when we begin at a level that provides context.

When we evaluate the social, political, and economic systems in which we live—which is essential if we are to construct a more just and sustainable world—we will find ourselves often trying to ask very detailed questions, drawing on the theories and tools from specific disciplines. But in doing that, we should always try to understand our complex world from three standpoints:

- Philosophically: Seeking knowledge and truth that is (potentially) universal.
- Historically: Recognizing the different ways people over time have understood human nature and organized their societies.
- Sociologically: Identifying patterns in the distribution of power in our society today.

Philosophy has many branches and can be approached in many different ways. But the word, from the ancient Greek, simply means a love of wisdom or knowledge. The quest to expand our knowledge and develop wisdom is rooted, at least for me, in the elusive search for truth, in the most expansive sense of that word—true for all people in all places at all times. Perhaps that desire is unhealthy, but I can't seem to shake it. The possibility of that kind of universal truth is intoxicating.

But we have too many examples of people who, drunk on the belief that they had found that universal truth, imposed it on others in brutal fashion. So we also need always to be thinking historically, recognizing the myriad different ways that human truth claims have played out over time. Even if we might want to proclaim some assertions as true, history teaches that there are different ways to live a truth. Only with a sense of history can we responsibly manage that desire to understand what may be true about ourselves, our society, and the world.

Finally, we also should always be thinking sociologically, a term I use here to describe the search to understand patterns in a society's distribution of power and wealth. We use gender, sexuality, race/ethnicity, social class, and other identity categories not simply to identify and/or celebrate our differences, but to understand where real power lies and how it operates. We are interested in understanding who is in charge of determining and pronouncing the truth, because those who hold that power typically control resources.

Just as the first set of questions about identity reminds us not to focus merely on ourselves in understanding identity, this set of guidelines reminds us not to focus on only one aspect of our reality. Although at any given moment we may focus on a narrow question that we try to answer in very specific ways, we always want to return to thinking at multiple levels. The answers we find to narrow questions matter only when placed in a larger context.

As we work to understand ourselves in those contexts, we also move among different types of inquiry with different goals:

- Empirical: Producing data through our inquiry.
- Analytical: Organizing that data in meaningful fashion.
- Normative: Articulating social norms to guide our lives.

In empirical work, we search for the facts, the data on which we build our attempts to describe the world. We recognize the tentative nature of human understanding—even when it comes to relatively simple assertions of fact, we humans are working on sand, not bedrock. But the facts matter, and though our methods are imperfect we don't abandon the quest to build the most trustworthy databases possible. This empirical inquiry can take the form of an experiment or observation, reported as "qualitative" data that offers descriptions of the world in words or "quantitative" data that creates categories with words and then uses numbers to report results within those categories.[2]

Whichever form of inquiry and whichever style of reporting is used, this data is "information organized for analysis." While the empirical inquiry may tell us things that are interesting on their own merit, we typically collect data toward the goal of analysis, our attempts to explain how the world works. Those analytical efforts can include physicists' attempts to explain the fundamental rules of the physical universe or political scientists' attempts to explain how voting patterns in a particular election correlate with income. Since analysis is built on our always tentative determination of the facts, our claims about how the world works will be tentative as well.

Coming to understand how the world works does not answer deeper questions of how we should organize human societies and what rules should guide those societies. Every human community establishes social norms, the rules that govern behavior, and so in addition to making claims about the world as it is, we will make normative claims about how we believe the world should be. A rule against cheating on an exam is a normative claim, based on an argument about what education is for and how we can best educate students. A democratic political system is based on a normative claim about how power should be distributed.

Although we are identifying these three levels of inquiry separately, they are connected in some important ways. We may want to tell a simple story about how we collect facts, analyze those facts to offer our best explanations, and then use those explanations to inform our judgments about how best to construct social norms. But it's never that simple. The existing social norms in a society or group will affect which questions we ask and how we understand the relevance of the questions. The existing analytical framework we start with will affect how we go about looking for empirical evidence. There is interplay between all these aspects of our investigations into, and assertions about, the world. As the Talking Heads song puts it, "Facts all come with points of view."[3]

One more way to say this: No knowledge is pre-theoretical. We can never engage the world without some existing idea about how the world works that will guide our inquiry, what we might call a "theory." We can't collect data without an existing theory about the question we are seeking to answer. The way we think about a question organizes the way we go into the world to answer that question. Like all the other cautionary reminders about the contingent nature of our knowledge, recognizing this doesn't mean there is nothing we can know, but simply reminds us that nothing is simple.[4]

I have waited to use the terms "theory" and "theoretical" until now, to avoid the confusion that comes from how those terms get used in everyday language. When someone says, "That's just a theory" to counter a proposed explanation, what they typically mean is "There are not strong reasons to accept that particular theory as our best explanation." In conversation, "just a theory" usually translates into "I think you're wrong."

All theories, in this sense, are just a theory, just a proposed explanation. Some theories are well supported, others more speculative. Given the limits of our knowledge, all theories should be offered tentatively, but the contingency of our understanding doesn't mean it's all just opinion. Over time we develop ways of testing our theories, both through formal scientific methods and informal practical ones. Some theories are better supported than others.

This comes up in contemporary culture most often around the theory of evolution by natural selection. Critics, usually citing religious beliefs, contend that it's "just a theory." Fair enough, but the real question is how compelling a theory it is. We know that evolution happens; we have plenty of evidence that organisms experience genetic change over generations. What is the best way to explain that evolution? The vast majority of biologists, and lots of other laypeople who have studied the subject, have concluded that the theory of evolution by natural selection is the most compelling explanation and that no other explanation yet offered is plausible. That doesn't mean that a new theory might not emerge in the future that is more compelling, but it does mean that of the theories on the table today, evolution by natural selection is by far the strongest.

More recently, a similar debate has arisen around the role of human behavior in climate change. Virtually all climate scientists agree on the basics: The planet is warming because we are adding heat-trapping greenhouse gases to the atmosphere, primarily by burning fossil fuels. While exact predictions are impossible, we can expect rising sea levels, more extreme weather, and other changes that will disrupt business-as-usual for humans. That's a theory, which means that, as with any theory, it could be wrong in part or whole, but it is the strongest theory we have today. That so many people reject that theory says more about the deniers' politics and theology than it does about an evaluation of the evidence.[5]

This is the nature of human inquiry—always exciting in what we learn and always frustrating in the limits of what we can know. This is captured in the philosopher Karl Popper's definition of theory, these systematic attempts at explanation that we humans create: "Theories are nets cast to catch what we call 'the world': to rationalize, to explain, and to master it. We endeavor to make the mesh ever finer and finer."[6]

Complex questions await when one delves deeper into the philosophy of science or the specific methods of a discipline. Making the mesh finer is both wondrously, and maddeningly, complicated. My goal has been to sketch an approach to intellectual work that is simple without being simplistic, that captures the potential and the limits of our knowledge. From here, we will confront the inevitably political nature of our attempts to understand the world.

CHAPTER 3

Power Basics:
Political but More than Politics

If democracy begins in conversation, as the political philosopher John Dewey often suggested, then we want to foster a culture in which ordinary people routinely talk in public about religion and politics—about those foundational issues concerning how to understand ourselves in relation to the world, and how to distribute power and resources. That public conversation is bound to be contentious, but it can be constructive when we engage each other as critically thinking intellectuals. If that conversation is to go beyond just spouting opinions at each other, we need to be able to make normative claims that we can support and that others can take seriously. Those claims should be based on empirical evidence we can trust and analysis that is sound, all rooted in good intellectual practices that are collectively maintained.

In the highly charged partisan atmosphere of the contemporary United States, many people not only are frustrated with the contentious nature of much of the mass-mediated debate over these questions but are deeply distrustful of all claims being made. Students routinely tell me that they don't believe anything that anyone on any side of these debates says, that they assume everything is skewed by people's political positions—in short, that it's nothing but politics, implying a dishonest and untrustworthy process. I hear the same complaint from older folks as well. If people believe there is no way to find any solid ground on which to base a political position, then political discourse rooted in rationality appears to be impossible. The problem is not simply that people don't like conflict but that they have lost faith in the possibility of honest argumentation in public and hence lost faith in finding an honest way to resolve political conflict.

Especially in a hyper-mediated world that treats everything—politics, art, sports—as mass spectacle entertainment, such disgust with the level and nature of debate is easy to understand. But our fatigue with a degraded culture doesn't eliminate our obligations as citizens. We still need to come to our own normative judgments, especially about how to distribute power and wealth, and discuss those options collectively to decide on public policy. When we aren't part of that process, others speak and act for us, and we often don't like what they say and do. Unless we want to abandon our world to the very people we believe to be the least trustworthy among us, we need to be critically thinking intellectuals.

These concerns about political partisanship and intellectual integrity are crucial to the quality of our public debate, but they also raise a more basic question. If we are worried not just that political spinmeisters knowingly falsify evidence and bend logic, but also that well-intentioned folk end up skewing the world to fit their own politics, we may wonder whether we can trust ourselves. Everyone has a theology and a politics—even those who have no interest in such matters base their lives on some assumptions and assertions about what people are and how society should be organized. All of us have some foundational understandings of what it means to be human, which we use to build our worldview, our way of understanding ourselves in relation to others and the living world. If other people's critical thinking might be swayed by their theology and politics, as they sometimes clearly are, then it stands to reason that my own could be similarly affected.

There are several common ways people handle this challenge. Some simply ignore the questions and keep asserting that their own knowledge claims are obviously superior to the opponents' claims. This is a common response of political partisans who strive to carry the day simply by force of will, rhetoric, or power.

Others acknowledge the questions and offer themselves as knowledge specialists who can transcend the political sphere by following special procedures and practices. Mainstream journalists, university professors, and independent researchers in a variety of fields routinely offer their services to society as professional sources of knowledge who can be trusted precisely because their professions are designed to remove them from political struggles. They claim to be neutral and non-ideological.

A more sensible position is to recognize that our knowledge seeking is inevitably shaped by our theological and political commitments, a situation that is simply a part of being human and not a reason to abandon hope of defensible intellectual practice or retreat into false claims of neutrality and life beyond ideology. While there's a theology and a politics undergirding everything we claim in an argument, those claims can be more than "just politics."

Neutrality

Is neutrality necessary to find truths we can defend? Should we expect intellectual specialists to be neutral when they communicate the truths they believe they have found? The questions assume that neutrality is possible, that there is a vantage point from which a person can observe the world free from political, moral, or theological values; and that we can communicate to others in language that is value-free. Neither assumption holds up.

First, the question of point of view. No one is, or can be, a neutral observer of the world. Take a simple example of eyewitness testimony. Imagine that a scuffle breaks out between two men on a crowded street corner. One of the men is white, middle-aged, and wearing a suit, while the other is black, younger, and wearing casual clothes and a hooded sweatshirt. There is pushing and shoving, voices are raised and insults exchanged, a gun drops to the ground, and the young man runs away. Police arrive to take a statement from the ten witnesses, all of whom had an equally clear view of the incident. Who started the altercation? What was the nature of the fight? What was said? Which man had the gun?

Will all ten statements be the same? Not likely, based on what we know about memory fallibility. Would the inevitable discrepancies between the witnesses have anything to do with their politics? It is plausible that the witnesses' views about race and class might influence their perception of the incident, without any of them even being aware of those influences. Can we train ourselves to transcend our assumptions?

The question makes sense only if we believe we can live without any assumptions. Certainly we can learn to identify and assess our assumptions—that's part of critical thinking—but we cannot live in the world as truly blank slates.

Every attempt to gather information to understand the world is based on an understanding of the world and how it works. Again, no knowledge is pre-theoretical. When we are trying to understand people and societies, every inquiry comes with a set of assumptions about the nature of human beings, relations among humans, and the place of humans in the larger world. There is no neutral ground on which to stand to view the world.

This is compounded when we describe the world to others using language, which also undermines our attempts at neutrality. To make this point in my class, I put on the screen a simple sentence with a request that students fill in the blank:

"Columbus _____ America."

When I was a grade-school student in the United States in the mid-1960s, we filled in the blank with "discovered," but today that word would be hotly contested. If we say Columbus discovered America, we imply that other humans had yet to set foot on the island of Hispaniola, since a claim to discover something is a claim to be the first person to arrive. But Columbus found the island inhabited by the Arawak-speaking Taino people. Suggesting that he and the other Europeans with him discovered America is to suggest the Taino were not fully human, not capable of discovery. To use the word "discovered" in this context, then, is racist and ethnocentric. There is a politics to the choice of "discovered."

Sometimes students will respond that "discovered" is just shorthand for "was the first European to discover." But if that's what is meant, then why not use the full phrase? Is it really crucial to save those five words? And if that is the case, would we be just as likely to describe the first indigenous Americans' trip to Europe by saying those folks discovered Europe? Even in the most charitable interpretation, the claim that "Columbus discovered America" is European-centric, and that is a political stance.

When I ask students to suggest another term, some come back with "conquered," "colonized," "destroyed," or similar terms. A strong case can be made for choosing such words, but they just as clearly have political implications, primarily a judgment that the actions of Columbus and other Europeans were immoral, illegal, or illegitimate in some fashion. There are obvious political judgments in the choice of those terms.

Students then offer a variety of terms that, on the surface, seem to avoid judgment: "encountered," "engaged with," or—my favorite of all the ones ever offered in class—"stumbled upon." But those words, despite the appearance of neutrality, also carry a politics. I offer the students an analogy: Suppose some folks from another neighborhood roll into your part of town, make their way through the houses of you and your neighbors, steal everything of value, and kill or work to death everyone. Would you say that those newcomers "encountered" or "stumbled upon" your neighborhood? Such a seemingly neutral term would obscure the violence, and therefore would favor the marauders.

Moving forward from that historical example, consider any number of contemporary choices. Is waterboarding "torture" or "enhanced interrogation"? One term suggests criminal and/or immoral activity, the other an action that is legally and morally permissible. Both are political, as would be any word created for the action; even new words we might create in an attempt to be neutral would eventually come to carry a judgment through the way they would be used.

Should the U.S. military action in March 2003 be called "the Iraq War" or "the U.S. invasion and occupation of Iraq"? The former implies a legitimate conflict, the latter an illegitimate intervention. Was the federal legislation passed in the wake of the 2008 financial meltdown a "rescue package" or a "bailout"? Again, whatever word one chooses, it will carry political connotations. Perhaps the most often cited example of this is the recurring debate about whether members of a political group that uses violence, including violence against civilians, are "terrorists" or "freedom fighters." People will argue for one or the other of these terms, or opt for other choices. The only thing we can say for sure is that all are politicized terms.

This does not mean that we should give up on any attempts to identify and understand the effects of our preconceived notions when we collect data about the world; such self-reflection is a part of good intellectual practice. In our attempts to report the results of our inquiry, we should avoid language that skews the case for or against a proposition based only on emotion or existing prejudice; such a commitment to honest communication is also part of good intellectual practice. The fact that there is no neutral place to stand does not mean we should not do our best to be honest in our attempts to gain knowledge and convey that knowledge to others. It just means we shouldn't be naïve.

Ideology

The desire for knowledge untainted by theological or political commitments also is expressed in the claim of some people and professions to being non-ideological. To evaluate that claim, the first step is to define the term, which is routinely used in three different ways.

The first is ideology-as-insult, probably the most common use of the term in everyday language. When someone suggests to another, "don't be so ideological," an ideology is understood as a belief system that is abstract, rigid, impractical, or fanatical. People using the term this way typically are suggesting that an ideology is something other folks have, which keeps them from seeing things clearly. The assumption behind this view is that there is a commonsense way of interpreting the world without resorting to a reality-distorting ideology.

We have all been in discussions where it seemed clear that the other person was not trying to look at all sides of a question but simply pressing a position out of an unreflective commitment to a belief system. If we were to be honest, we could identify times in our lives when we exhibited the same rigidity. So, if we all have the capacity to get lost in our ideology, who exactly are those people we can trust to have the undistorted commonsense vision? The fact that we all know people who argue fanatically and seem incapable of real dialog—people we tend to label "ideologues"— should not lead any one of us to think we have the crystal-clear, non-ideological view.

The second definition is ideology-as-worldview. This more sociological perspective understands ideology as the set of social, political, and moral values, attitudes, outlooks, and beliefs that shape a social group's interpretation of the world.

Understanding ideology as the framework within which we make sense of the world, it's clear that everyone has an ideology or ideologies. The assumption here is that there is no neutral inquiry into the world.

When the word is defined this way, it's difficult to argue that anyone is non-ideological or beyond ideology. Rather than hurl the label at others as an insult, this definition encourages us to think not only about other people's frameworks but about our own. By suggesting we develop our ideologies as part of a social group, this definition also encourages us to look at the larger context in which our views develop, rather than see them as the product of a purely individual effort.

The third definition is ideology-as-power. This critical view understands ideology as the beliefs of a ruling group, which are imposed on a subordinate group so as to make the ruling ideas appear to be self-evident. From this perspective, ideology is a tool of the powerful that obscures the truth of social relations. The assumption in this case is that ideology should be critiqued to help people better understand their real place in society and resist injustice.

Many people identify this view of ideology as Marxist, the view that a ruling class in capitalism uses its control over the ideological institutions (schools, universities, churches, mass media) to maintain this dominance and allow it to govern without the need for continuous coercion and violence. A similar argument is made by some feminists analyzing male dominance, or critical race scholars and activists analyzing white supremacy. In most cases, these critics don't suggest that the dominant group's ability to control ideas is so powerful that it cannot be resisted, but simply that those in charge have more powerful tools at their disposal.

In some sense, all three definitions are accurate. People, on any side of an issue, can fail to see how they are caught in an ideological box that prevents them from recognizing evidence and analysis that challenges their views. We can counter that self-indulgence by recognizing that we all have an ideology, or ideologies. And we can at the same time realize that all ideologies do not come with the same force behind them, and that sometimes an ideological box is constructed by people in power to try to keep the rest of us trapped.

We can see some aspect of all these conceptions of ideology in this excerpt from the congressional testimony of Alan Greenspan. Many believe that Greenspan, who was chair of the Federal Reserve of the United States from 1987 to 2006, bears much of the blame for the 2008 financial meltdown. Although he rejected responsibility, Greenspan did acknowledge that some of his assumptions about how the economy works—and his predictions about the effects of his policies—proved inaccurate. In this exchange, California Democrat Henry Waxman raised a question about Greenspan's ideology:

> **Waxman:** The question I have for you is, you had an ideology, you had a belief that free, competitive—and this is your statement—"I do have an ideology. My judgment is that free, competitive markets are by far the unrivaled way to organize economies. We've tried regulation. None meaningfully worked." That was your quote. You had the authority to prevent irresponsible lending practices that led to the subprime mortgage crisis. You were advised to do so by many others. And now our

whole economy is paying its price. Do you feel that your ideology pushed you to make decisions that you wish you had not made?

Greenspan: Well, remember that what an ideology is, is a conceptual framework with the way people deal with reality. Everyone has one. You have to—to exist, you need an ideology. The question is whether it is accurate or not. And what I'm saying to you is, yes, I found a flaw. I don't know how significant or permanent it is, but I've been very distressed by that fact. . . .

Waxman: You found a flaw in the reality?

Greenspan: Flaw in the model that I perceived is the critical functioning structure that defines how the world works, so to speak.

Waxman: In other words, you found that your view of the world, your ideology, was not right, it was not working?

Greenspan: That is, precisely. That's precisely the reason I was shocked, because I had been going for forty years or more with very considerable evidence that it was working exceptionally well.[1]

The exchange starts with Waxman suggesting that Greenspan's overly zealous commitment to free-market ideology, with its presumption against government regulation, had led him to advocate policies that contributed to the melt-down. Greenspan reminds Waxman that ideology is not a slur but simply a way we organize our thinking. What is left unsaid is that that the dominance of free-market ideology—not only in Greenspan's worldview but in the whole culture—is the product of years of efforts by the corporate sector to make that free-market view the common sense of the society.[2]

Greenspan is simplifying a bit too much when he says the question is whether an ideology "is accurate or not." Some ideologies prove to be based on more accurate data and more compelling interpretation of data, but no ideological framework can guarantee a correct answer to every question in such a complex world. Better to say that some ideologies do a better job than others in guiding our actions, but that in the end no ideology completely captures the world.

Teaching and politics

This complexity doesn't mean we should abandon our quest to understand the world, but rather reminds us that we shouldn't pretend that we can transcend our ideological framework and find a neutral place from which to understand the world. Instead, we can work to cultivate our ability to be critically self-reflective, so that we can evaluate the ideologies of others and be more aware of our own.

Applying this reasoning to my job as a university professor, I put it this way: All teaching about human affairs has a politics, but teaching is more than just politics. In the classroom my goal is not to persuade students that my political judgments are correct but to pose challenging questions and encourage critical thinking. Rather than feigning neutrality or pretending to be beyond ideology, I try to make visible the political implications of the class, which are reflected in every decision I make. Why did I organize the course this way? Choose these textbooks? Lecture on these specific topics? Highlight these points of view? Most faculty members have years of professional training that guide us in these decisions, but the decisions can't be reduced to purely professional judgments.

Every professor's politics come into play, but it's not always obvious how professors' politics influence a class. When instructors' politics reflect the dominant culture's conventional wisdom, they look apolitical. To teach a course in the United States that is based on the assumption that capitalism is the proper way to organize an industrial economy appears neutral and beyond ideology. To teach a course that assumes socialism is the proper system will appear politicized. Both courses are political, in the sense I'm using the term. Either course might be taught badly or taught well; in either course the professor could inappropriately harangue students and demand that they adopt the professor's view. That's bad teaching, not because a professor's politics are out in the open but because the professor is undermining the students' critical thinking.

Here's another example that works particularly well on my campus. In the class before a football weekend, I will tell students that I hope they will boycott the game as a protest against the way in which big-money intercollegiate athletics undermines the integrity of the university as an intellectual institution. After a pause, I ask if anyone thinks that statement inappropriately injects my political views into the classroom. Many agree that it does. Then I pose this question: If I had ended the class with a suggestion that they show some school spirit by going to the game and helping cheer the Longhorns to victory, would anyone have accused me of inappropriately politicizing the classroom? Probably not, because on our football-obsessed campus such sentiments are the norm, and one hears the pro-football position stated over and over. Yet both statements are equally politicized assessments of the athletic program, one critical and one supportive.

As a teacher, I reject both the retreat to illusory neutrality and any assertion of aggressive advocacy. My goal is open and honest engagement with students based on critical self-reflection and mutual respect. As the professor, I clearly have more power than the students and therefore have to be careful not to undermine their critical thinking. But I can do that best by making visible my ideology and, when appropriate, explaining the evidence and reasoning that led me to adopt these positions.

I tell my students that they can expect three different modes of address from me during a semester. Sometimes I will present relatively uncontroversial information that is the consensus of scholars in the field. Other times, when scholars disagree, I will survey the different interpretations, presenting each view as accurately as I can while making my own position clear. And there are times when I will present to the class a proposition and make an argument for it, presenting my evidence and reasoning. I do that to model the process of critical thinking, which is so rare in our public political discourse. I tell students their job is not to accept my position but to think about the assumptions I am making, definitions of terms, quality of the evidence, validity of the logic, and soundness of the argument.

My one overtly political goal in my teaching is the desire to politicize students who are depoliticized, to encourage them to apply their intellectual skills to the political world not just to understand but to participate. I offer them the often quoted line from Socrates: "The unexamined life is not worth living," which I supplement with a less well-known quote from the U.S. political activist and theologian William Sloane Coffin Jr.: "Socrates had it wrong; it is not the unexamined but finally the uncommitted life that is not worth living."[3]

CHAPTER 4

Thinking Critically about Politics

There's a temptation when offering examples of critical thinking to look for relatively easy issues that will alienate as few people as possible. I would rather wade into questions on which there are strong feelings and deep divides, in the hopes of making good on the claim that honest critical engagement is possible. In this chapter, I'll look at one particularly thorny question in politics, the relationship of the political and economic systems, and then examine one common way bad arguments are framed, typically to marginalize dissent.

Democracy and capitalism

It's striking how we routinely talk about politics and economics separately, as if they exist in different worlds. Yet it's clear the two systems cannot be understood independently of each other. Politics creates the structure for an economy, and the distribution of wealth in an economy affects politics, a simple observation that has important implications for contemporary democracy. Although there has been more discussion of this since the U.S. Supreme Court's 2010 decision in the *Citizens United* case,[1] which expanded the ability of corporations and wealthy individuals to influence elections, the conversation is typically about relatively superficial changes in campaign finance law, not about the fundamental question of whether democracy and capitalism are compatible.

We can start by pointing out the absurdity of the claim that we should "get the government out of the economy," which is impossible. Without government—that is, without rules that are the product of collective action through government—the modern economy could not exist. The laws governing contracts are the product of governmental action, as are the laws creating the modern corporation. Beyond those obvious building blocks, it's unlikely that any of the high-tech components of the modern economy—from the first machine-tooled parts developed for the military in the nineteenth century to today's computers, robotics, and internet—would have gotten off the ground without government subsidies for early research and development.[2]

From the most basic institutions of the economy to policies that affect specific industries within the economy, government is always mixed up in business. We can argue about which policies are best, but arguing that the government should get out of the economy is nonsensical. Such a claim typically is used to camouflage attempts to press for government rules that favor particular individuals, corporations, or industries. There is no pre-political or pre-regulatory status quo that we can look to as the way things would be if not for government interference, nor can we pretend that the existing economy could have been created without substantial government funding. As economist Joseph Stiglitz puts it:

> Any economic system has to have rules and regulations; it has to operate within a legal framework.

There are many different such frameworks, and each has consequences for distribution as well as growth, efficiency, and stability.[3]

Just as obviously, the way in which the economy distributes wealth will affect people's ability to participate in the political process. Consider the similarities and differences between me and Bill Gates, whose fortune is estimated at around $50 billion. Bill and I have exactly the same legal guarantees of freedom of expression and association—we both can pretty much say what we want about politics and gather with others to pursue our political interests. Bill and I both can petition our government for a redress of grievances, and in the voting booth we each get one ballot. Therefore, Bill Gates and I have the same opportunities to affect politics, correct?

We all laugh at such a notion, for the obvious reason: Bill Gates's fortune allows him to buy the means to amplify his voice through mass-media advertising; to contribute to political campaigns to win access to lawmakers; to pay lobbyists to advance his interests in state and national legislatures. About the only moment when Bill and I are political equals is when we step into the voting booth, but by that point the game is already fixed in his favor. The point is simple: The concentration of wealth affects the distribution of power. In a nation where the top 1 percent of the population controls 35 percent of the wealth and the top 20 percent of the population controls 85 percent of the wealth,[4] we can't talk about political equality without talking about economic inequality.[5]

I developed a classroom exercise that provides students with a short but powerful experience of this. I divide the class of about 200 students into the top 20 percent and bottom

80 percent. As a stand-in for money, I use the space in the classroom. I tell the 40 students in the wealthy category that they will have 85 percent of the seats, while the remaining 160 students must share 15 percent of the seats. In that classroom, which has 320 chairs, those 160 have to make do with 48 seats and the surrounding aisles. While the 40 "elite" students have plenty of room to stretch out and relax, the "commoners" are squeezed together uncomfortably, most of them standing. Playing the role of the government enforcing the law, I bark at the commoners when they dare to venture out of their allotted space.

To those commoners, I pose this question: How would you react if I tried to persuade you that, even though you were going to be stuck in this situation for the fifteen weeks of a semester, you were going to have the same educational experience as the elite? You will all listen to the same lectures, read the same textbooks, take the same exams and be graded on the same standards. Therefore, you all have the same chance at getting a quality education, correct? The commoners don't accept that claim, for the obvious reasons that the one way in which they are different from the elites—the physical space to participate effectively—makes all the difference in the world.

I make it clear to students that the exercise is not premised on a judgment about whether this distribution of wealth is consistent with anyone's moral principles, which is a crucial question but one separate from an evaluation of wealth inequality on political participation. The exercise is meant to highlight a central question that is routinely ignored: Are our economic and political systems compatible? The United States' corporate-capitalist economy exists alongside the democratic institutions of the U.S. republic. But does the concentration of wealth in the economy undermine the possibility of meaningful democracy in the political arena?

This question may sound strange in a society in which capitalism and democracy are not only assumed to be compatible, but many would argue they are the same thing: Market systems are based on individual choice, and democracy is based on individual choice; therefore capitalism is democracy. That argument may seem plausible when confined to the pages of a basic economics textbook, but it evaporates quickly in the real world.

One of the ways people try to derail this discussion is to suggest that a critique of capitalism is tantamount to an endorsement of Soviet-style communism. This is a classic example of one of the most potent ways to undermine critical thinking—presenting false alternatives.

False alternatives
An argument based on false alternatives keeps people from considering the full range of relevant possibilities. Typically, this involves presenting an issue as if there are two—and only two—possible courses of action, one of which is unattractive for practical and/or moral reasons. An argument from false alternatives also routinely builds into its claim one or more assumptions that could be challenged.

One common example is "love it or leave it." If a citizen objects to a public policy, especially involving a war, someone who supports that policy will suggest the opponent should love the country or get out. Since most people aren't going to abandon their home—"leave it" just isn't an option—it appears they have no choice except to "love it," which is defined as supporting the policy. Such a suggestion is not only anti-intellectual but anti-democratic. Obviously, people don't have to choose between loving their country no matter what policy is followed or getting out. We can love our country and want to change a government's action, such as a war, because we believe that would make it a better country. In a democracy, that kind of critique not only is allowed but should be encouraged—it is, in fact, the lifeblood of politics. Demanding that people "love it or leave it" is a way to undermine critical thinking and democratic dialog by ignoring all the other possibilities. Unconditional love might be appropriate in certain human relationships, but it is not conducive to a healthy intellectual and political life.

The "love it or leave it" claim also sneaks in an assumption—that loyalty to one's country should be the highest value, that patriotism is a virtue. But there are other ways people can define their moral and political identity that would argue against the unstated claim that one's first loyalty is owed to a nation-state. What if one believes the nation-state leads to an unacceptable concentration of power? What if one identifies with the larger human family and universal principles rather than with the concept of a country or nation-state? Or a specific religious tradition and a community of believers, or a bioregion and the local inhabitants? There may be a good argument for a primary loyalty to country, but it shouldn't be assumed.[6]

Another example of a classic false alternative in politics is the demand that we choose between "special interests" and the "national interest." In the contemporary United States, this comes up routinely in discussion of domestic policy, especially policy involving expenditures of government funds. The game being played is simple: You try to identify your political opponents as representing special interests (presumed to be selfish, a negative) and fuse your position with the national interest (always presented as selfless, a positive).

Depending on the politics of the person making the argument, the special interests being targeted may be large corporations angling for tax breaks or labor unions advocating for increased wages and benefits. Historically, those with wealth have done their best to paint themselves as working in the national interest (even though they are the minority) and their opponents as representing special interests (even though they are the majority). But whatever the specifics of the issue or the proposal, the special-versus-national-interest framework is always an impediment to deeper understanding of an issue for a simple reason: There is no such thing as "the" national interest.

Try to imagine a policy that would be equally beneficial and/or acceptable to all 300 million people in the United States. Take a basic issue, such as the structure of the tax code. Should the federal government collect revenue through an income tax? If so, should it be a flat tax or a progressive tax? What should the tax rate be? In a society with large disparities in income and wealth, no answer is in the national interest. The "nation" is those 300 million people, and any answer will benefit some more than others. We can assume that an attempt to identify a specific choice with the so-called national interest is likely to be pushed by those benefiting from that choice.

This doesn't mean that some choices might not be better than others based on specific criteria, that some choices don't benefit many more people than others, or that people should support only those policies that benefit them directly. Wealthy people could choose, for example, to support a tax code that benefits working people out of a sense of justice. But we should debate proposals on their merits rather than an empty claim about the national interest.

Such a debate allows us to examine not only the technical details of a tax proposal, but the underlying moral and political assumptions—rejecting the deceptive special-versus-national-interest framework promotes more rigorous intellectual inquiry. Sticking with tax policy as an example, one justification routinely offered on behalf of a specific tax policy proposal is that it will stimulate economic growth. If we don't get trapped by seductive slogans, we can inquire about the evidence for the claim; about what kind of economic growth is likely to result; and about whether that's the kind of growth we want. We might even question whether economic growth itself is preferable, given that a growing economy often means degraded ecosystems.

I have been challenged on this claim that there is never a single national interest that all citizens of a nation could endorse. What about the threat of foreign invasion? Wouldn't repelling such a threat be in the national interest? Certainly in some cases it might be possible to get a near-unanimous agreement from citizens, such as in the case of an invasion by a vicious fascist state such as Nazi Germany. But less clear-cut cases are easy to imagine. For instance, what if in the 1850s Mexico had invaded the southern United States? One can easily imagine that some in the United States, most notably those enslaved, might welcome an invasion by a country that more than a decade earlier had outlawed slavery. If an existing government oppresses its people, foreign invasion may be a preferable option.

Politics is hard

One particularly dangerous example of how false alternatives can undermine critical thinking and political engagement is the often repeated claim that "if you don't vote, you can't complain." This cliché suggests that to be politically relevant, one must get involved in electoral politics through support for a candidate or a political party. People who don't participate in that system can expect to be accused of being apathetic and bad citizens. A vibrant democracy does depend on the involvement of ordinary people, but does that mean we must choose between participating in the electoral process or being politically irrelevant? Only if we accept the assumption behind this false alternative—that the only meaningful politics comes in the electoral arena.

Some might suggest that since in our system the elected representatives make and enforce the laws, electing those representatives is the most important way to participate in politics. But history teaches that ordinary people are most effective politically when they join together outside of electoral party politics to form popular movements aimed at putting pressure on whoever happens to be in those elected positions.

People involved in grassroots organizing to build power are an important part of participatory democracy. If people choose to focus their time and energy on those popular movements, they aren't apathetic or bad citizens. Whether one approach is more effective than the other in any particular place and time can be debated. But organizing both within and outside the electoral system is all political, if we understand politics as the struggle for how power will be distributed in a society. Those who insist that voting is the primary, or even the only, way to participate are trying to direct citizens toward a particular form of political engagement without providing an argument for why that particular form will be most effective.

This is not an abstract question. In the United States, the rules of our electoral system favor the two established parties, and hence the people in control of those parties have an interest in the status quo. If real grassroots organizing is a threat to that system, then it's not surprising that people in power would prefer we all channel our political energy into the elections that they dominate, or into "safe" non-profit groups that will support the status quo.[7]

When challenging people to think about politics in this more expansive fashion, a common response is frustration. How can we make sense of these complex issues when more and more of the political talk we hear is less and less substantive? All of this critical thinking about politics is hard enough when one has access to clear and coherent arguments from multiple perspectives, but in our society most of the critical perspectives that challenge the systems and structures of power are not regularly represented in mainstream politics. Republicans and Democrats certainly have differences over policy—and sometimes over basic philosophy—but both parties support that system and those structures. News media have a tendency to present views outside that mainstream as irrelevant at best, or crazy at worst. Searching the margins for critical ideas is not simple, either; just because powerful institutions and people reject an idea doesn't mean the idea is automatically compelling.

All this is complicated, but one thing seems clear: When people try to figure it out all on their own, they are bound to fail. I remember as a young person bouncing between points of view, picking up ideas that seemed intriguing but were in the end inadequate, all in intellectual and political isolation. We expand our vision not only through acquiring information but by engaging with others. In the process of that engagement, we are led to new information and alternative interpretations. I didn't start to construct a coherent political worldview until I got involved in politics, through grassroots groups.

Many people respond to that with "That's fine for you, but I'm not political," which is based on the flawed notion that one can live outside of politics. We are all political, whether we become politically active or not. We all live in a society in which there is a distribution of power. If we don't participate in politics at some level, we are simply handing our latent political power to others to exercise for us. As difficult as it can be to come to judgment about complex issues, to avoid making a judgment simply gives someone else the power to judge for you.

That's true about politics. It's also true about religion.

CHAPTER 5

Thinking Critically about Religion

As difficult as it is to think critically about politics and engage others in discussion about those topics, most people have even more trouble with religion and theology. That may be because our views about religion seem even more personal, and hence critique seems more dangerous. Religion also involves statements about faith, or statements about the world that are rooted in faith—both of which leave us uncertain about how to respond to others, especially when we find their faith experiences disconcerting.

But just as we should adopt a more expansive view of politics, we should think of theology as taking us beyond the doctrines of any specific denomination or faith tradition. Because politics is about the distribution of power, we all have a politics; if we don't articulate a political point of view, we are likely just accepting the politics of the dominant culture. If religion struggles with the basic questions of how we humans understand ourselves and our place in the world, then we all have a theology, whether it's rooted in conventional notions of a deity, in non-theistic religious traditions, or in secular philosophies. We're all operating in our daily lives based on some set of answers to those questions, however tentative our answers may be.

Finally, many argue that religion is a private matter and need not be part of the larger cultural dialog. But if we understand religion and theology more expansively, then there is no way to bracket it out of our collective conversation, since our views on those fundamental questions have a direct effect on how we resolve public policy. That means our critical thinking about religion has to be truly critical—we need inter- and intra-faith debate. If that debate goes forward with respect and rigorous intellectual standards, we all will improve our understanding not only of others and their beliefs, but of ourselves and our beliefs. Such discussions are not a threat to anyone's religious faith but a way to deepen it.

In this chapter I offer some critical thinking about two specific questions that come up frequently in the United States, especially within the dominant Christian tradition, and then reflect on what all this means for intellectual life.

Does God have a gender?
In contemporary Christianity (and in many other religious traditions), it is common practice in most churches to refer to God using the male pronoun. Feminist and other critically minded people have challenged this practice, and some congregations and some versions of the Bible have shifted to non-gendered language. Still, the more common practice is to treat God linguistically as male. There are endless debates among scholars about how to translate specific words from the original Hebrew and Greek texts into other languages, but that is not the discussion I want to enter into.

Let's start with the recognition that the Hebrew Bible

and the Christian New Testament are patriarchal. Whether one considers patriarchy to be positive (because God and/or biology dictate such a system) or negative (because it is an oppressive system maintained by force and coercion), both those texts emerged from patriarchal cultures—systems in which men take the dominant roles in public and private life, claiming that their dominance is not arbitrary but natural and necessary. So it's hardly surprising that patriarchal language is common.

Rather than start with the question of gender, this inquiry is more productive if we begin with questions about the basic nature of God. When I have discussed this with those who support using male pronouns for God, I ask a simple question: Is God, as you understand the concept of the divine, a name for a being or entity that is in any way like a human person? Everyone agrees God is not a person or like a person. Then I ask, is God some other kind of animal or creature that we would recognize as having either male or female sexual characteristics? Everyone agrees God is not such a creature.

At this point, it doesn't really matter what one means by the term God. Is God a definable entity of any kind? Is God the name for the force behind all living things? Is God simply another name for the mystery of the world beyond our comprehension?[1] Whatever one's answer, it's clear that God does not fit into the male/female category as we understand it for creatures like us, and we do not have the capacity to define exactly what other category God fits into. If most of those who identify with the Christian tradition believe God to be beyond our human capacity to understand, then asking whether God is male or female is a bit like asking whether God has curly or straight hair, is tall or short. It's not that the questions are hard to answer, but rather that the questions simply don't make any sense. Whatever God is, God isn't that kind of thing. Projecting onto God such human characteristics could be seen as a form of idolatry.

So why does God need to be male or female? The answer seems pretty clear: In a patriarchal society structured on male dominance, images of an ultimate power are likely to reflect the distribution of power in the society. As philosopher Mary Daly put it in the early years of the second wave of the U.S. feminist movement, "[I]f God is male, then the male is God."[2] Such a society is likely to project onto any understanding of God a male identity, even while acknowledging that God doesn't have a sex. If the goal is to deepen our understanding of God, a good first step might be to leave behind the need to assign a gender.

The most common defense of the God-is-male position is textual, rooted in the belief that clear understandings can be extracted from scripture and that, in this case, the male pronoun for God comes from God through that sacred text. This approach—a belief that a text can be read by the faithful in a way that generates definitive truths—is not unique to Christianity. In a confusing and complex world, the promise of such clarity is seductive. But all that comforts us does not always hold up when we engage in critical thinking.

Can a sacred text be understood literally?

Several years ago I had an ongoing conversation with a young man who was an evangelical Christian. One day the discussion turned to biblical interpretation. He attended a church in which people believed that the Bible had plain meaning and that anyone who applied common sense could know that meaning with relatively little disagreement. From their perspective, the Bible is the word of God and therefore completely inerrant in all aspects or, at least, infallible on matters of faith (I was never clear on which position he held), and God gave us the ability to read and understand without the inherent ambiguity and potential confusion that comes with all other human communication.

So, I asked him, would you and the folks at your church say that there is no interpretation of the text necessary? Yes, he said, we take the Bible literally and don't interpret. Then I asked him about the different kinds of writing in the Bible. There are historical accounts, articulations of divine law, moral teachings, parables, poetry—the Bible speaks in different voices, in many types of literature, yes? He agreed.

I asked him: Do you read the poetry the same way you read the accounts of history? Do you try to understand the parables the same way as a statement about law? Of course not, he said, because each had to be assessed according to the type of writing and the purpose of the passage. So is it fair to say, I continued, that you have an "interpretive strategy" for how to read different parts of the Bible differently depending on the type of writing? He agreed.

"So what you are contending," I said, "is that you read the Bible with an interpretive strategy, shifting your approach depending on what part of the Bible you are reading, but that you don't interpret the Bible?" He offered no clear response, and that turned out to be the last time he dropped by to talk. He may have taken offense at my question, but it was not meant disrespectfully. When two people disagree, making clear the nature of the disagreement is a mark of respect for the intellectual abilities of the other person. I wasn't arguing that his interpretation of any particular passage was wrong, only that his interpretation was just that—an interpretation, which couldn't simply be asserted as obvious and correct but had to be defended, just like any other interpretation. I had posed an honest question, one he had trouble answering.

This same discussion happens in every faith tradition, as well as in secular settings where people seek to understand any type of literature. Can there be a reading of any text that is beyond interpretation? If so, how do we resolve disagreements about any one person's claim to a definitive reading? Our desire for clarity may lead us to want a source of ultimate understanding that can reveal unchallengeable truth to us, but we're better off accepting that the best we can do is work hard to grasp truths, aware that a definitive understanding is always just beyond our grasp.

The conflict between fundamentalisms and intellectual life
The appeal to literalism is an aspect of what is commonly referred to as fundamentalism. In early twentieth-century Protestant history, the term was coined for a back-to-basics movement to promote "The Fundamentals"—doctrines asserting the inerrancy of scripture, virgin birth, Christ's death as atonement for sin, bodily resurrection of Christ, and historical reality of Christ's miracles. More generally fundamentalism can be used to describe any intellectual, political, or theological position that asserts an absolute certainty in the truth and/or righteousness of a belief system. In this sense, fundamentalism is an extreme form of hubris—overconfidence not only in one's beliefs but in the ability of humans to understand complex questions definitively.

Fundamentalism isn't unique to religious people but is

instead a feature of a certain approach to the world, rooted in mistaking limited human knowledge for complete wisdom. There are national fundamentalists who are convinced of the inherent righteousness of their nation-state; economic fundamentalists who believe that markets always know best; and technological fundamentalists who assume that high-technology gadgets are the solution to everything, including the problems created by high-technology gadgets. All fundamentalisms assume that one perspective can provide unquestioned authority, which is why all fundamentalisms are a threat to critical thinking and a healthy intellectual life.

But the fundamentalism that consistently attracts the most attention is religious. In the United States, the predominant form is Christian. Elsewhere in the world, Islamic, Jewish, and Hindu fundamentalisms are attractive to some significant portion of populations, either spread across a diaspora or concentrated in one region, or both. Rather than explore the social and political implications of religious fundamentalism, I want to ask the question most relevant to this book: Is a fundamentalist religious faith compatible with critical thinking? That is not irreligious or disrespectful of the value of spirituality and faith, but merely asks a question the culture would prefer to ignore: Can one be a critically thinking person in the sense I have been describing, and also be a fundamentalist?

This question should be of particular concern in public universities but is rarely discussed, I think because the religious fundamentalism of a significant chunk of the population is at odds with the critical thinking at the core of public education. I hear about this struggle from students who come from fundamentalist homes and find that university education is challenging their most basic assumptions about how to understand the world. Again, this is not about criticism of any specific religious doctrine, but about the basic approach to knowledge. These students recognize that their intellectual life will be constrained if they hold onto fundamentalist beliefs about the nature of truth and language.

There are two basic tensions between fundamentalism and a modern university. First, one of the foundational principles of the university is that everything—every theory, every argument, and every bit of evidence—is up for grabs. A corollary is that there have to be some generally accepted rules for defending evidence, arguments, and theories.

In an open intellectual atmosphere, nothing can be assumed to be true. A theory about the nature of the cosmos or the proper functioning of government—or the nature of the divine—can never be taken to be definitive and final. There may be such overwhelming evidence for some theories at a particular moment that we build certain practices and institutions on their explanatory power, but no case is ever truly closed. The history of inquiry is a history of change in ideas and understandings; being an intellectual means accepting that what we take today to be the obvious truth is likely incomplete and quite possibly wrong. Another aspect of intellectual life is being willing to subject one's arguments to critique from others, following shared rules about how that critique should go forward. Those rules are always open to challenge, but some endure, such as the expectation that evidence has to be accessible to others. In an intellectual argument, one can't simply demand that another person accept evidence without a chance to examine it. So when a person adopts a theological position based on a faith experience, that experience provides a basis for the individual's choice. But while faith experiences can be described to others, and patterns in faith experiences can be evaluated, a faith experience is not evidence in the sense we use that term in intellectual life—it can't be replicated or presented to others to examine. A claim that a particular theological doctrine is true beyond questioning, backed by evidence for that truth from a faith experience, may be a compelling claim for people who share the faith experience. But it doesn't provide the basis for intellectual engagement.

My point is not to single out religious fundamentalism as posing a unique challenge. Rather I hope that the clear conflict between religious fundamentalism and critical thinking helps us see the threat posed by those other fundamentalisms. In many of those other cases, the threat is not only from students who hold onto a fundamentalist worldview but from professors who embrace those other fundamentalisms. What about national fundamentalists teaching government and history who assume the sacrosanct status of the "founding fathers" and their cause? What about economics professors who teach market fundamentalism? And what about a technological fundamentalism that not only dominates in the sciences but is widespread across disciplines? Critical thinking demands we challenge them all.

Religion matters
These arguments do not target a particular faith tradition, or only religious people. This chapter doesn't try to stake out a claim on specific doctrinal issues, but rather explores some of the ways we approach religion and theological questions,

which should be of interest to us all. Those who identify as atheist or agnostic should be just as interested in how we collectively struggle with the foundational questions about ourselves and our place in the world.

I resist the claims that some of the faithful make to have found definitive answers, but I resist just as strongly the notion that if religion can't make such claims it is irrelevant or purely personal. I reject attempts to impose any public policy based on religious claims that are asserted as definitively true, but I also reject the notion that religious views should play no part in our debates about public policy. Religion, just like secular philosophy, is a vehicle for struggling with those basic questions about what it means to be a human being—as an individual, in relation to others, and in relation to the larger living world. People have struggled, and will continue to struggle, with those questions in a variety of ways, and all can contribute to our collective attempt to find answers—as long as we agree to do it based on rules for intellectual practice that produces the best critical thinking we're capable of generating collectively.

My stress on "collective" and "collectively" is intentional, not just because we are all in this together, but because that is how we come to understand the world, as part of a collective enterprise. A capitalist economic system asserts that humans are autonomous individuals always seeking to maximize self-interest, and that individualistic approach seeps into the entire culture. But we are, of course, social animals, not just in the ways we socialize but in the ways we think and feel our way through the world. In our increasingly mass-mediated world, that means that thinking critically about storytelling and news media is more important than ever.

CHAPTER 6

Thinking Critically about News Media

Perhaps the one thing that unites most Americans is their disgust with, and distrust of, journalism: Everyone hates the media. Surveys show that less than one-third of Americans say that news organizations generally get the facts straight, and the level of trust is dropping.[1] Much of this distrust is expressed as a belief that journalists are not objective and, therefore, have become a vehicle for propaganda.

As is often the case, these critiques typically are made with no clear definition of "objectivity" or "propaganda." In this chapter I will offer some suggestions about definitions, not with the expectation that everyone will come to agreement about journalism but in the hope that such disagreements will be more productive.

Objectivity

Like most terms, "objective" and "objectivity" are used in different ways in different contexts. In everyday conversation, if someone is making an argument that seems to be unfairly skewed or unnecessarily argumentative, we often counsel that the person to "try to be objective." What we typically mean is that the other person's passion or prejudices might be impeding their ability to see things clearly. Being objective, in this case, means something like this: Try to understand your preconceived ideas about the subject and recognize how those preconceptions might skew your perspective, even to the point that you may be tempted to fudge the facts or make claims that aren't true. When we ask each other to be objective, we are reminding ourselves to keep an open mind and not shade the truth or make things up just because they bolster our argument.

In that everyday sense of the term, objectivity is a good thing—for me, for you, for journalists, for everyone. Objectivity is just another way of reminding ourselves what good intellectual practice looks like. To be objective, we need not pretend we don't have a point of view, that we aren't passionate about our ideas and commitments. Rather, the reminder to be objective is a corrective if our passion leads to sloppiness in our critical thinking.

Objectivity also has a more specific meaning in the context of a scientific laboratory. Scientists don't claim to have developed a method that brackets out all subjective decisions; science is an enterprise carried out by humans. But the scientific method offers a way to generate knowledge that can be rigorously tested and verified. Scientists develop protocols for measuring aspects of the world they wish to study and devising experiments to test hypotheses. These methods are not foolproof, but they have been extremely successful in expanding our understanding of the world.

This scientific sense of objectivity may guide our intellectual practices—we adapt ideas about measurement and experimentation in rough fashion to our everyday life. For example, if we want to know whether a dish we've cooked tasted better with or without hot peppers, we might conduct an ad hoc experiment by preparing the food both ways and asking our dinner guests which they prefer. Journalists also do this, but not with the kind of rigor that one sees in a laboratory. Scientific objectivity, in the strict sense, isn't possible in journalism.

Neither of those definitions captures what objectivity means in mainstream corporate-commercial journalism in the United States today.[2] Yes, journalists strive to be objective in the everyday sense, and when possible journalists mimic the method of scientists. But "objectivity" in practice in mainstream journalism defines a set of professional practices that are most concerned with who is a trustworthy source and where those sources hang out. This practice of objective journalism—which favors what are typically called "official sources" from officially sanctioned institutions—actually undermines the ability of journalists to do their job responsibly.

While journalists move about in the world and sometimes directly observe events they write about, much of journalism is based on other people's accounts of what happens. Journalists get this information through interviewing people or reviewing documents that others have produced. The crucial question for journalists is which people and which written accounts are most authoritative? When there are conflicting accounts of the world, which can be trusted? The research on this subject,[3] and my own experience as a working journalist, points to a simple conclusion: Official sources dominate the mainstream news. An official source, in journalistic practice, is someone associated with a reputable organization that has some credibility and status in the culture. In the contemporary United States, that usually means the government and the corporation, and a few other institutions that are seen as producing trustworthy knowledge, such as universities and think tanks. These become the "authorized knowers" on whom journalists rely.

Here's an example of how journalists rely on these sources. After many of the claims made to justify the U.S. invasion of Iraq in 2003 were demonstrated to be false, journalists were challenged to explain their failure to provide a critical and independent evaluation of those claims during the run-up to the invasion. One such exchange took place on *The Daily Show,* with Jon Stewart questioning CNN anchor Wolf Blitzer. After acknowledging the failure, Blitzer explained that he and other journalists had done the necessary reporting but still were unable to learn the truth:

> So, I remember going off. I had all the briefings. I went over, got the briefings from the CIA, the Pentagon, spoke to all the members of Congress, the intelligence committees, the House side, the Senate side. Everybody said the same thing: There is no doubt there are stockpiles of chemical and biological weapons, and it's only a matter of time before he has a nuclear bomb.[4]

Note the sources that Blitzer includes in his list of "all the briefings" that were important in reporting the story: His sources were all officials from the U.S. government. Those officials don't really constitute "all" of the potential sources, of course; Blitzer is suggesting that they are all the relevant sources. But might there have been others who could have provided information and analysis that questioned the U.S.

claims about Iraq's weapons programs? What about sources in the anti-war movement in the United States, including former government officials who were warning that the claims were overblown? Or independent sources in the Middle East who might have firsthand knowledge? Or sources who could speak to past cases in which government officials lied about a foreign threat to justify war?[5]

Blitzer's reflexive defense of his reporting is common in mainstream journalism. This reliance on official sources may not always produce good journalism—and sometimes may produce truly reprehensible journalism—but it's easy to understand why the practice continues. Using official sources takes less time; government and corporate officials have large public relations operations that produce information in formats journalists can easily use. That information is presumed credible, and journalists don't have to defend their reporting techniques to news managers, since that's the way it has always been done. This means the news managers can hire fewer reporters, reducing labor costs and increasing profits. And because most journalists think of themselves as working in a profession, in the same kind of position as lawyers, for example, there is a subtle class allegiance at play—when evaluating sources, it's not surprising that journalists favor folks whom they view as being similar to them in education, social class, and worldview.

While we shouldn't accept the claim that journalists' professional practices produce objectivity, we also shouldn't assume that the production of news is a totally subjective enterprise based on the whims of individuals. Journalists work within a system, interacting with political actors who are also working within systems, all responding to the people reading and watching the news. Rather than ask whether any one person in these systems is objective or subjective, we should understand news—like all human knowledge—as the product of an intersubjective process. The relevant questions are about the power each group has to affect the direction, framing, and content of the news. These officials are not only sources whom reporters quote in news stories but also news shapers; they play a key role in defining what counts as news.[6] When representatives of the wealthy and powerful have a disproportionate influence in that intersubjective process, the news is skewed toward the perspective of those forces and tends to marginalize dissident voices, which reinforces the ideology of the powerful and helps make that ideology appear to be the "common sense" of the culture by virtue of its constant repetition. These conventional reporting practices absorb the ideologies of the official sources but do not make it explicit.

One last warning about how words are used: As "objectivity" became increasingly suspect to more and more news consumers, some journalists have abandoned the term and begun describing their goal as "fairness." While it's healthy for journalists to recognize that naïve notions of objectivity are counterproductive, what's needed is a shift not just in the term but in the underlying practices. If the professional practices that were described by "objectivity" don't change, then relabeling them as "fairness" changes nothing. The problem isn't the label we use to describe the practices, it's the practices themselves.

Critiquing these professional routines is central to understanding journalism, just as an evaluation of the practices of other professionals such as lawyers is part of understanding the role of law in society. Assessing journalism also requires that we look at the effects of the corporate-commercial structure of the mainstream news media and at the larger ideological framework within which journalists work. Two important critics of the news media have argued that these forces create a journalism that often serves a propaganda function for the powerful.[7] To make sense of that claim, we need to think clearly about what we mean when we describe a message as "propaganda."

Propaganda and persuasion

Propaganda is another term frequently used but rarely defined with clarity. The term originates in the seventeenth century as part of the Catholic Counter-Reformation, when the Sacred Congregation for the Propagation of the Faith was charged with spreading doctrine in response to the Protestant challenge. Until World War I, the term was used to mean any attempt to spread information and was not generally seen as pejorative. During that war the United States created its first official state propaganda agency to manipulate public opinion toward support for a generally unpopular war, and the term began to acquire a negative connotation. By the end of World War II, the successful propaganda efforts of the Nazis solidified that association of propaganda with communication strategies designed to undermine people's ability to participate in the honest and open dialog essential to democracy. Today, to label someone's communication effort as propaganda is understood as criticism.

But because democracy is based on people routinely trying to persuade each other to support proposals, it's not enough to define propaganda as a systematic attempt to convince others to endorse a political idea or project. How can we distinguish between attempts to persuade that are consistent with good intellectual practice and democracy (what we might call democratic persuasion), and attempts to manipulate people that are inconsistent with good intellectual practice and democracy (what we might call undemocratic propaganda)? The distinction is not as easy to make as we may wish it were.

Consider the definition offered in a widely used textbook by two contemporary scholars: "Propaganda is the deliberate, systematic attempt to shape perceptions, manipulate cognitions, and direct behavior to achieve a response that furthers the desired intent of the propagandist."[8] I often give public talks about political subjects. In those speeches, I engage in a deliberate, systematic attempt to affect my audience's perceptions, cognitions, and behaviors. If they don't agree with me, I want them to change their minds. If they do agree with me, I want to solidify their position. In doing this, I don't mention every possibly relevant fact or put forward every interpretation of those facts; I select the evidence and arguments that I think most important. Inevitably, I shape and, in some sense, manipulate. Is that propaganda? Working from that definition, it's hard to tell.

When I pose this question to my students—is there a principled way to distinguish persuasion from propaganda?—some common answers emerge. First, they say, propaganda is lying, the knowing use of false statements to support a position. Certainly some of what we understand to be propaganda includes false statements, but much propaganda isn't about claims that are clearly true or false, but about interpretation and impressions. Second, students suggest, propaganda uses emotion to manipulate people. Again, that's often the case, but is emotion not part of how we understand the world? If any appeal to emotion to influence people is propaganda, then there would be no role for our emotional reactions in public life, making for a sterile and inhuman public discourse. Third, propaganda exploits powerful images to override rational thought. But does that mean photography and film are not legitimate ways to present information about the world? If images always override our critical capacities, then we're in real trouble.

I have not found, nor been able to construct, a definition of propaganda that can distinguish with precision the propaganda we want to avoid from the persuasion that is part of democratic dialog—such are the limits of language when dealing with the messiness of human affairs. But the attempt to clarify these concepts matters, because democracy is based on deliberation that, at least in theory, can produce resolutions of policy disagreements that are acceptable to all. In a democratic system we don't hold out for the unrealistic goal of everyone agreeing about everything, but rather ask everyone to commit to a process that produces a fair resolution based on an honest and transparent process. If propaganda is a useful term to mark the communication techniques that derail that process, then we should struggle to deepen our understanding.

Rather than searching for a precise definition, I will offer a list of features of systems that intuitively we think of as healthy persuasion and unhealthy propaganda, drawn from a variety of sources.

Democratic persuasion involves these factors:

- serious effort to create background conditions that give

each person access to the resources needed to fully participate in discussion;

- serious effort to create forums in which access to the
  discussion is based not on power or money but on a
  principle of equality; and
- commitment of all participants to intellectual honesty
  in presenting arguments and a willingness to respond to
  the arguments of others.

Undemocratic propaganda involves these deliberate
actions:

- falsification of accounts of the world to support one's
  interests;
- attempts to ignore or bury accounts of the world that
  conflict with one's interests; and/or
- diversion of discussion away from questions that would
  produce accounts of the world that conflict with one's
  interests.

There is one disturbing implication of this approach: It
suggests that virtually all commercial advertising and a significant portion of our political discourse is propaganda, or at
least at some level propagandistic. From this perspective, the
advertising, marketing, and public relations industries would
be described collectively as the propaganda industries. When
we consider how much our social environment is influenced
by those industries, we would hesitate to speak glibly about
living in a democratic political system and a free society. When
journalists become the transmission vehicle for much of this
material, we might hesitate to speak glibly about a free press.

What do we say about the state of our political discourse when a presidential campaign can win the advertising industry's "marketer of the year" award, as the Obama campaign did in 2008?[9] What do we say about a democracy in which a president's chief of staff, when asked why the Bush administration waited until after Labor Day to launch its campaign to convince the American public that military action against Iraq was necessary, says, "From a marketing point of view, you don't introduce new products in August."[10]

We are left to ponder the degree to which deception, distortion, and distraction have become not perversions of an otherwise healthy public discourse but the perverse norm of that discourse. That question is disturbing, but rather than undermine our commitment to critical thinking, it should spur us to be more creative and courageous.

CHAPTER 7

Thinking Creatively:
Paradoxes, Metaphors, Aphorisms

This book has focused so far on conventional notions of argumentation in which we try to identify assumptions, define terms, present evidence, and argue for a clearly articulated proposition. Those skills are especially important as the complexity of our world intensifies and the increasingly entertainment-obsessed culture ignores the need for this kind of careful thought process. But we also need to recognize that critical thinking comes through many doors, and that we can open up new ways of thinking through other styles of engagement.

Paradoxes

Precisely because the world is complex, we often face issues that require us to see things from multiple perspectives at one time. Presenting questions in paradoxical form can help us see the complexity and, if not resolve it, at least struggle to deepen our understanding.

As children, most of us stumbled upon a version of the liar's paradox. To tease, someone says, "You can't believe anything I say because I always lie." If that statement is true, then I can't believe the statement; there is an apparent contradiction in the speaker's claim. If that statement is true, then whatever the speaker says is false, including that statement. The liar is lying about being a liar. The practical resolution of the paradox is simple: The claim is not serious. No one lies all the time, or tells the truth all the time. The paradox is resolved by a simple reality check.

There are more difficult logical and mathematical paradoxes that require sophisticated analysis, but my interest here is in paradoxes that arise out of our everyday lives and challenge us to rethink our assumptions. Here's one I ponder often:

We are most free when we are most bound to others.

On the surface, that appears to be a contradiction. If freedom is understood as the ability to act without the constraints that come from external forces, then we are most free when we have nothing binding us—freedom is the absence of potential restrictions, what philosophers refer to as "negative liberty."[1] If we are bound to others, then we would seem to be more constrained, less able to make free choices. When politicians throughout history have contended that people find "freedom" in their allegiance to a nation, party, or glorious leader, we are rightly skeptical; telling people to subordinate themselves to the greater good in that fashion sounds a lot like fascist rhetoric.

This understanding of negative freedom will resonate with anyone who has ever lived under a hierarchical political system that imposes arbitrary constraints. There is no way to be free when we do not control our own bodies and actions. The lack of freedom in those situations—everything from conditions of literal slavery, to the ever-present monitoring of individuals in a totalitarian society, to stifling restrictions on civil liberties in an otherwise democratic state—makes it impossible for people to be fully human.

One important articulation of this notion of freedom, the harm principle, comes from John Stuart Mill: "[T]he sole end for which mankind are warranted, individually or collectively, in interfering with the liberty of action of any of their number, is self-protection. . . . [T]he only purpose for which power can be rightfully exercised over any member of a civilized community, against his will, is to prevent harm to others."[2] This principle, which in our society we grasp intuitively, is simple: We should be free to do anything so long as it does not harm another.

The harm principle assumes that we are fully autonomous, self-contained beings who should view our relationships from that point of view. That may be a necessary assumption when we think about our relationship to the state, which claims the right to use force and coercion to enforce its rules. In the case of laws made by government, the harm principle might be a good anchor. There will inevitably be disputes about what constitutes a harm of sufficient gravity to warrant collective action, but the basic principle is clear enough.

But what of our understanding of freedom not just in political terms but also in social and economic arenas? The examples of classic constraints on freedom—slavery, totalitarianism, restricted civil liberties—come through laws of governments. But we also live our lives in social groups and workplaces, which are structured and affected by government actions but also are separate spheres.

Socially: While most of us can, and do, choose to move

in and out of various social groups in our lives, should we understand ourselves in social terms as separate individuals making choices? Are we distinct individuals who join groups to fulfill needs that we have determined on our own? Or is it more accurate to think of ourselves as constituted by our membership in groups? We don't bring a fully formed identity into our connections to others but construct an identity through those connections. We are, in a very real sense, who we hang out with. That doesn't mean we have no capacity to make our own decisions, or to decide on a course of action at odds with the groups to which we belong. Our goal can be to maintain a sense of individuality (a recognition that each of us is unique and has a creative capacity) while giving up individualism (the naïve belief that we exist as fully autonomous beings separate from social groups).[3]

Economically: In a capitalist world with large and growing gaps between rich and poor, what sense does it make to speak of individuals making free choices? The distribution of wealth in our society is structured by centuries of inequality, during which elites used state power to enrich themselves and create structures—especially the modern industrial corporation—to concentrate wealth further. Those inequalities are hardened by ongoing elite domination of politics as well as deeply entrenched social patterns. In such a world, are people really free? Why do most people feel the least free in their working lives?

So, in our social worlds, it becomes hard for any of us to understand ourselves as autonomous individuals; it's not the kind of beings we are. In our workplaces, most of us are disempowered if we think of ourselves as autonomous individuals; it simply reinforces the power of the boss. The question isn't whether we are bound to others—we are, it's the human condition—but how we understand our identities and interests, which is about how we understand power. Rather than imagining we can cut those ties that bind, we should focus on the people to whom we're bound, and through what institutions. Some of those connections help us be the free, creative beings we are capable of being, and some keep us trapped in relationships that constrain us.

When we ask questions about freedom in the abstract, assuming that human beings are completely rational and completely autonomous, we come up with inadequate understandings of freedom. To suggest "we are most free when we are most bound to others" sounds ridiculous if we are working with those assumptions. But when we recognize that we cannot escape each other—that human life without those bonds is at best an impoverished life, and at worst no life at all—then we can see our freedom as being rooted in those bonds. This view doesn't mean we must capitulate to the hierarchies of government, social groups, or corporations, but rather encourages us to explore what kinds of collective living allow us to express our individuality without destroying the connections to others that not only make life worth living but make life possible.

Metaphors

The figures of speech we call metaphors work through the association of unlike things to make a point and deepen our understanding. Some metaphors are so common that we don't think much of them. When we say we are going to "dive into a project," for example, we don't mean we literally will go into a body of water to work on a project, but rather that we are going to immerse ourselves in that work. Some metaphors are more foundational, such as "life is a journey," which reminds us of how our lives unfold in unpredictable ways as we move toward a destination.[4]

Many philosophers of language and mind suggest that we not only express ourselves using metaphors but think metaphorically. As is often the case, specialists debate the finer points of that claim, but whatever the results of those debates it is clear that metaphors can shape our thinking about a subject; our choice of metaphors is more than just stylistic. Researchers have found that metaphors can have a powerful influence over how people attempt to solve complex problems. For example, in one study people offered very different responses to questions about crime depending on the metaphor used—either a "beast" or a "virus" ravaging society—and were not aware of the influence of metaphor on their thinking.[5]

Consider the number of times the U.S. government has declared "war" on a social or health problem (poverty, cancer, drugs). How does that metaphor, which suggests an all-out effort to vanquish an enemy, direct our attention? Fighting a war on poverty focuses on helping those suffering because of wealth inequality, not on challenging those riding high or the system that produces the inequality. The war on cancer has been concerned with finding a cure rather than highlighting the effects of a toxic environment on cancer rates and advocating that we reclaim the health of ecosystems. Is a war that has targeted not only dealers but drug users—leaving hundreds of thousands of people, disproportionately black and Latino, in prison and jail[6]—really the way to deal with drug addiction?

Today, as we face multiple ecological crises, what metaphor for the trajectory of the human species on the planet would help us understand our future—where are we heading, how are we getting there, how long will it take? Some people suggest we are a car speeding toward the cliff, while others suggest the car is about to run out of gas. Water metaphors come up: A canoe on a river heading for a waterfall, or a boat in the middle of the ocean that is leaking badly. The different metaphors open up conversation—as people explain their reasons for choosing a particular metaphor, they can discuss the scope of the crises, the nature of the challenges we face, and the time available to make corrections.

My preferred metaphor to illuminate crucial social, economic, and ecological issues starts with imagining the modern world as a train. A product of the industrial revolution, powered by fossil fuels, a train allows people to travel distances in a matter of hours that would have taken days, weeks, or even months on foot or with animal power. Traveling on modern trains in the First World is generally comfortable—with seats that recline for a nap, lights to make reading possible, a dining car if one is hungry. Life on the train is pretty good, especially if one is riding in the first-class car. That is where the social and economic issues arise.

When we are riding in our First World first-class car, someone else is doing the work that allows us that comfort. Those laborers are riding in cars at the back of the train, in more crowded and sometimes dangerous conditions. Some of those laborers are invisible to those of us in the forward cars, while others may come into our car to serve. What are the working and living conditions for those people? For those of us who are living comfortably in the affluent First World, those questions are easy to ignore if we so choose.

But no matter who is riding in which car of the train,

there are ecological questions about the very nature of the train. When the metals and fuels for the railroad were first extracted from the Earth, no one thought about how long the ride could continue—resources were treated as if they were inexhaustible. But how much longer can we extract those metals and fuels before they run out? And what of the toxic waste that goes into the water, land, and air as a result of the consumption of those resources? As our train speeds by, what do we leave in its wake?

If using all these resources to operate the train has created ecological crises, and those resources also are running out, it might make sense to slow down the train and start planning for the changes that are inevitable. But in the contemporary world, that's not happening. We're on a runaway train,[7] with no one in the conductor's car, no one in charge thinking clearly about the condition of the train. Given the complexity of the modern global economic and political systems, there is no single conductor's car, no one person who could make a decision to slow down the train.

How will this end? If the train continues running at a speed greater than the system can handle, it will derail. If the resources for maintaining the system dwindle and repair work is not done in a timely fashion, it will derail. Shouldn't we be asking critical questions: Wouldn't the best action be to slow the train down and rethink the whole project? Why are we speeding forward? Why are some people serving those in the first-class cabin but living in the equivalent of a cargo car?

If those questions aren't taken seriously in the dominant culture at the moment, what is a person of conscience supposed to do? If we see that in the first-class car at the front of the train the passengers are consuming and wasting the most, should we walk further back in the train, where people are living more modestly? Environmentalist David Orr has dubbed this "walking north on a southbound train."[8] Consuming less and wasting less is a good thing to do, but we are still part of a society that is moving forward at an unsustainable speed. Individual actions to live more simply are intrinsically good, but they won't stop the train. Orr's metaphor reminds us of the need for radical change in the system. If enough people decided to figure out how to slow the train, it's possible there is time to avoid derailment. The longer the train speeds forward without change, the closer we get to derailment, and the more extreme the measures needed to avoid catastrophe.

There's no need to exhaust the metaphor; any one metaphor does not provide the perfect map to untangling a problem. Rather than expecting a metaphor to provide answers, we explore it to help us understand the problem. As Arturo Rosenblueth and Norbert Wiener, pioneers of field of cybernetics, said, "The price of metaphor is eternal vigilance."[9]

Aphorisms

An aphorism—an insightful observation expressed in short, memorable form—can be a great tool in sparking critical thinking. Aphorisms, like metaphors and paradoxes, don't settle complex questions but can open doors to new ways of thinking, ones we might not have previously been aware of. Their power comes not in definitively proving a claim, but from the ideas generated out of them. The best aphorisms grab us and demand that we pay attention.

Here's an aphorism that got my attention, from Bruce Wright, a political scientist retired from California State University, Fullerton:

The universe is an undifferentiated whole. About that we can say nothing more.

I first heard those lines cited by Bruce's brother, Angus—an environmental studies professor retired from California State University, Sacramento—during a discussion at the Land Institute in 2004, about the "ignorance-based worldview" mentioned in the introduction to this book. Recall Wes Jackson's suggestion that we should understand that the knowledge we humans can acquire—while impressive in what it allows us to build—is not adequate to manage the complexity of the world. No matter how smart we are, our ignorance will always outstrip our knowledge, and so we routinely fail to anticipate or control the consequences of our science and technology.

Bruce Wright's aphorism reinforces that point and takes it a step further: It's not just that scientific analysis can't tell us everything, but that the analytical process destroys the unity of what we are trying to study. When we analyze, the subject becomes an object, as we break it apart to allow us to poke and probe in the pursuit of that analysis.

To "differentiate," in this context, means the act of perceiving and assigning distinctions within a system. Thinking of the universe as an undifferentiated whole recognizes its unity, providing a corrective to the method of modern science that breaks things down to manageable components that can be studied. That "reductionism" in science assumes that the behavior of a system can be understood most effectively by observing the behavior of its parts. At first glance that may seem not only obvious but unavoidable. How else would we ever know anything? We can't look out at the universe and somehow magically understand how things work—we have to break it down into smaller parts.

Imagine a pond in the woods. That ecosystem includes air, water, and land; the various inanimate objects such as rocks; the plants we see and their root structures underground; the animals and marine life that are big enough for us to see and the many other micro–life forms we can't observe with our eyes; and the weather. No one person could walk into the scene and offer a detailed account of all that is happening in that ecosystem, let alone explain how it operates. Even a cursory description of the ecosystem requires knowledge of meteorology, botany, zoology, geology, chemistry, physics. To make sense of the complex relationships and interactions among all the players in that one small ecosystem, experts in those disciplines would observe, experiment, and explain their part of it. Putting all that knowledge together, we can say some important things about the system, but we can't claim to know how it really works. Not only is there a unity to the ecosystem that we can't understand, but our analytic approach destroys the unity we seek to understand.

Does that sound crazy? Consider two obvious limitations of our knowledge claims in science.

First, if we claim to understand the system through its component parts, we have to be able to identify all the relevant parts. How much do we know about the microscopic organisms and their role in that ecosystem? We know the things we have identified, using the tools we have at our disposal. But is that all there is to be identified, that which we can observe? For all that scientists and farmers know about soil, for example, most of what happens in the soil is at the microscopic level and unknown to us. Second, while that pond ecosystem can be broken down into its component parts and studied, that study cannot include the dynamic interactions between all the parts, which are too complex to track. It's not a failure of the method, but simply an unavoidable limitation.

In short, the whole is more than the sum of its parts, and considerably more than the sum of the parts we can observe. The process of scientific analysis—of studying the parts to try to understand the whole—is powerful but limited. When we take what we've learned about the parts and construct a picture of the whole, we will miss the complex interactions between all those parts, which are crucial in creating the whole.

There's nothing wrong with using methods that are limited—any method we employ will be limited. Scientists struggling with these problems understand the vexing nature of "complex adaptive systems," a term that recognizes we are dealing not with static parts but with dynamic networks of interactions and that the behavior of the entities will change based on experience. But problems arise when people make claims to definitive knowledge and then intervene in the world based on those claims, often with unpleasant results. Unintended consequences do damage that often is beyond repair.

Wright's aphorism suggests we should not only see a specific ecosystem as a whole, but regard the universe as a whole, as one big system of complex and dynamic interactions. While seemingly fanciful at that level, this idea has been widely discussed at the scale of the planet. To say that Earth is an undifferentiated whole is to suggest that everything in our world—organic and inorganic—can be understood to form a single self-regulating complex adaptive system. This is the Gaia hypothesis formulated by the environmentalist James Lovelock: The Earth itself is a living thing.[10] Whether or not one goes that far, it focuses our attention on the dynamic, complex, adaptive nature of our world.

Wright's provocative claim—"About this we can say nothing more"—doesn't mean that we can say nothing at all about the component parts, only that we can't pretend to say more than we can really know about the whole. To describe a system as an undifferentiated whole is to mark its integrity as a whole, something that must be understood on those terms. Once we see the world as a living system, our attempt to know it through analysis of the parts is, by definition, always an incomplete project. We can't really know the whole world; it exceeds our capacity.

CHAPTER 8

Thinking Courageously: Reframing Ourselves and Our World

Courage is typically associated with a willingness to take risks in action. Critical thinking can lead us to take risks when that thinking results in a challenge to widely held beliefs among friends, family, or community. The even greater risk in rigorous critical thinking is that we might have to abandon a position that has been central to our sense of ourselves; such thinking can result in an internal challenge to deeply held beliefs. This willingness to take intellectual risks doesn't guarantee that we will come to the correct answers, but cultivating the courage to think critically even when it is unpopular with others or unsettling to ourselves is important. It is crucial in a culture that seems unwilling to face its most serious problems around social justice and ecological sustainability.

In Chapter 2, I suggested that we should always be thinking about our identity at three levels: personal, societal, and ecological. I also suggested that in all our critical thinking, we should always be thinking philosophically, historically, and sociologically. In this chapter, I'll try to do that by tackling crucial contemporary questions about the ways we struggle to understand ourselves as individuals; as situated in a specific time and place, in a historical context; and as part of the larger living world.

Personal: It's just human nature

One of the most common, yet least compelling, arguments to explain human behavior is "It's just human nature." In fact, that's no explanation at all, and typically is an attempt to cover up a weak argument rather than defend an argument.

Obviously, anything humans do is by definition a result of human nature; if we do it, it's within our nature to do it. And given the range of human behavior—from the most hideous violence and cruelty that denies the humanity of others, to the most compassionate self-sacrificing actions taken out of solidarity with others—we can say that human nature is elastic enough to make possible virtually any imaginable act. Simply claiming that something we do is the result of human nature is an empty claim and diverts us from the more important question of the context within which human nature plays out.

An example: In my large lecture classes, I give multiple-choice exams, often in a crowded room where students sit side by side, making it easy to cheat. I assume some number of students will try to copy answers from the person next to them. In trying to understand the behavior, I could shrug and say, "That's just human nature"—in this case, to break rules to get something we want, such as a good grade on an exam for which we haven't studied hard enough. From that perspective, taking the violation of the rules as inevitable, my response might be to remind students of the importance of academic honesty, as I monitor them closely during the exam and punish violators. That response ignores the context and focuses on the behavior of individuals, not the design of the system.

The crucial question in this example isn't about human nature—again, since it happens, and happens routinely, it obviously is within our nature to cheat on exams—but about the nature of the setting in which students are choosing to cheat. Imagine a different classroom, with 25 instead of 250 students, all of whom have had an active role not only in class discussion but also in setting the goals for the course. Would students who helped create and maintain a more active learning environment be likely to cheat on an exam? In such a setting, would an exam even be necessary? The difference would not be that the students in one group had a different nature than the others, but that one experience was dramatically different than the other. The kinds of institutions within which we live are going to affect which aspects of our nature dominate.

The most important argument about human nature made today is in the theory behind contemporary capitalism, the claim that the inequality in our system is in the best interests of everyone. Capitalism asserts that because we are greedy, self-interested animals, we must reward greedy, self-interested behavior to create a rational and efficient economic system. Such a system is so creative and productive, the argument goes, that we should accept the inequality that results. Taken to an extreme, this view suggests this scheme is the essence of rationality itself: To be rational is to maximize one's self-interest, especially in the acquisition of material goods and services.

We all are capable, of course, of being greedy and self-interested. And we also are capable of sacrificing for others, including for strangers. Competition is part of human nature, as is cooperation. The argument for capitalism assumes that the competitive is the dominant part of our nature and will win out over the cooperative, and so it's better to design an economy around that assumption. But that remains an assumption until one provides evidence. What is the evidence? Look around, we're told, at how people behave. Everywhere we look, we see greed and the pursuit of self-interest. So the proof that these greedy, self-interested aspects of our nature are dominant is that, when we live in a system that rewards greed and self-interested behavior, people routinely act that way.

But is that always the case? Only if we confine our examination of human history to the last 10,000 years. Remember the trajectory of the genus *Homo* (which goes back a couple of million years) and the species *Homo sapiens* (200,000 years). For the first 95 percent of our evolutionary history, *Homo sapiens* lived in band-level societies defined by solidarity and cooperation, with high degrees of equality. Gift exchange and food sharing were the norm; greedy and self-interested behavior was detrimental to the chances for survival. Those gatherer-hunters died younger than we do today, but they worked far fewer hours.[1] We might ask, which system is more civilized?[2]

Tens of thousands of years ago, we became the dominant species on the planet because our natural capacity for maximizing individual self-interest was not primary. If greed is now the primary motivation, it's not because it's "natural"—in the sense of being the dominant part of our nature—but because institutions in the hierarchical societies that have arisen in relatively recent human history have rewarded that greed. Can we collectively make a commitment to reorder society along cooperative lines? In theory, of course, but it's not a simple task, given the rewards offered to those who dominate and control to maximize their own short-term material self-interest. The reflections of a lifelong political activist, Abe Osheroff, help put this in context.

In his ninety-two years, Osheroff made a living as a skilled carpenter and crafted a rich life as a political radical. Starting as a teenager in New York City, he organized tenants, the unemployed, and workers. In 1937 he joined the Abraham Lincoln Brigade, the U.S. wing of the International Brigades that attempted (but failed) to help protect the Spanish Republic against fascism. He continued to be active in progressive political organizing until his death in 2008. Although he was an astute observer of the human condition, Osheroff never wrote much, which led me to conduct an extensive interview with him and produce a documentary film about his ideas.[3] Below is a segment of that interview, in which Osheroff grapples with the questions of self-interest and solidarity.

> **Robert Jensen:** Cynical people say that people are naturally greedy, and so social justice is impossible. You reject that, but you've said that much of what you do is out of self-interest.

> **Abe Osheroff:** We have to get people to understand that it is in their self-interest to refuse to yield to that crasser kind of greed. Let me give you an example. When I lived in California, in Venice, we fought a land redevelopment project, a multi-multi-million-dollar project. We lost, but we held them at bay for about seven or eight years and protected that community for those years. These were very poor people living on the banks of shitty canals, but it was in

many ways a nice place to live, and it had a good community life. During that battle, a member of City Council offered me a bribe, two corner lots in the canals, which today would go for between $2 million and $5 million. They offered me a house built to my specifications. They offered me a dock and two boats, sail and motor. And I'll tell you, it took me a hard, painful night to turn that down.

RJ: If you had taken it, the deal would have been that you would abandon the organizing? And that was an offer you had to think about before saying no?

AO: That's it. I was the principal organizer in that struggle. And I did think about it. I was very tempted. It appealed to a side of me that wasn't totally gone. I'd love to get into a powerful position. I'd love to design the house I'm going to live in. I love the idea of my kids being guaranteed certain things. There's a part of me—it's not a big part of me, but I was surprised to find that it was still a part of me—that wanted all that shit. And if it's a part of me, with my politics and background, then it's a bigger part of a lot of other people. I could see that my real self-interest was with the people in my community, that was where love and affection come from, but it was tempting.

RJ: There are two different paths to go down here. One is to say to people, "Listen, I understand that you want all these material things, but if you put aside that greed there is something in the long run that will serve you better." Or you could say, "I know you want these things, but you have to train yourself not to want them because they aren't of any real value." Which is politically more effective and more realistic?

AO: You don't have to get rid of the instinct for material things to do this. You begin to practice, to learn that it's more rewarding to pursue a path that brings real love and affection. Everybody needs love. Everybody needs affection. Everybody needs validation. It's a central problem of human life, and very few people really get those things. . . . When I faced that bribe, I discovered there was a part of me that wanted the money, but luckily there was something else I wanted more of, something I had learned about through leftist politics. And I can articulate that now, even if I couldn't always: The only thing in human life you can give away and not be left with less is love and affection. It's simple, but not everyone understands this. If I give you some of my money, I have less. But if I give you love and affection, I don't have less, I have more. It's the only thing in human relations that is guaranteed to grow like that. I've learned that the hard way, and I still have things to learn about it. But that's at the center of what I try to teach activists—the importance of the role of love.

So what should we value more than material comfort? Love and affection, respect and validation.

I'm lucky because I'm bathed in it all the time, as a result of my political activism. And it's one of the big motivations for what I do. It's one of the things that keeps me going.

RJ: Will that sustain most people, or do the comforts of an affluent society obscure their ability to see that? It's pretty obvious that one of the reasons capitalism can continue at all is because it plays to that instinct in people. It's based on a certain conception of human nature that says we're all, in the end, greedy in the material sense.

AO: In some ways, that's right, of course. A lot can be done to make life different, to change the way we relate to each other, but I don't think we'll ever eliminate greed. The other side of it is they can never totally silence certain other forces in life, other parts of our nature. There will always be also in the human community—sometimes on a larger scale and sometimes on a smaller scale—a deep-seated resistance to greed as the dominant feature of life. Even without being political, people live that way, just out of being loving people.

Societal: Escaping the American Dream

In a world defined by nation-states, everyone's identity is shaped in part by citizenship. Whatever our relationship to the nation-state of which we are a part—whether we celebrate uncritically, resist that cheerleading, or reject the idea of nationality altogether—we have to define ourselves in relation to that political unit, which is foundational in the modern world.

While there will be a variety of ideas about that identity, there also tend to be dominant themes that define a nation-state. In the United States, one of those themes at the heart of people's conception of the nation, and hence of themselves, is the American Dream. A check in the library for books with that phrase in the title reveals a seemingly endless literature that describes and defines, analyzes and assesses the concept—everyone seems to be reviving, reinventing, redefining, remaking, recapturing, or rescuing the dream. Even when those examinations are critical of any particular style of dreaming, they typically offer up a positive dream interpretation toward which we can strive.

But the American Dream is, and always has been, inextricably bound up in domination, and there is no way to rehabilitate the dream if we want to make possible a just and sustainable human presence in a living world. Such a claim goes against the grain in the United States, and hence requires considerable explanation.

James Truslow Adams appears to have been the first to have used "the American Dream" in print, in his 1931 book *The Epic of America*. This stockbroker turned historian defined it as "that dream of a land in which life should be better and richer and fuller for everyone." But he didn't reduce the dream to materialism, emphasizing U.S. social mobility in contrast with a more rigid European class system:

> It is not a dream of motor cars and high wages merely, but a dream of social order in which each man and each woman shall be able to attain to the

fullest stature of which they are innately capable, and be recognized by others for what they are, regardless of the fortuitous circumstances of birth or position.[4]

Adams was concerned about the growing materialism of U.S. life, and he wondered about "the ugly scars which have also been left on us by our three centuries of exploitation and conquest of the continent."[5] Yet for all his concerns, Adams believed that the United States could overcome these problems as long as the dream endured, and that led him into the dead-end of clichés: "If we are to make the dream come true we must all work together, no longer to build bigger, but to build better."[6] For Adams, as the book's title makes clear, the story of America is an epic, and "The epic loses all its glory without the dream."[7]

The problem with this allegedly epic tale: That dream of a better, richer, fuller life for everyone in the United States is born of, and maintained by, domination; those "ugly scars" are not a footnote to the story but the core of the story. The United States of America can dream only because of one of the most extensive acts of genocide in recorded history, in which the European colonists and their heirs successfully eliminated almost the entire indigenous population—or the "merciless Indian Savages" as they are labeled in the Declaration of Independence, one of the most famous articulations of the American Dream. Those millions sacrificed were followed by millions more who died as a result of African slavery, which further enriched the American dreamers. And once powerful enough to project itself onto the world stage, the United

States turned from domination of the continent to domination of the globe.

Adams pointed out that while this is always about more than money, the idea of getting one's share of the American bounty is at the core of the American Dream. That bounty did not, of course, drop out of the sky. It was ripped from the ground and drawn from the water in a fashion that has left the continent ravaged, a dismemberment of nature that is an unavoidable consequence of a worldview that glorifies domination.

"From [Europeans'] first arrival we have behaved as though nature must be either subdued or ignored," writes Wes Jackson.[8] As Jackson points out, our economy has always been extractive, even before the industrial revolution dramatically accelerated the assault in the nineteenth century and the petrochemical revolution began poisoning the world more intensively in the twentieth. From the start, we mined the forests, soil, and aquifers, just as we eventually mined minerals and fossil fuels, leaving ecosystems ragged and in ruin, perhaps beyond recovery in any human time frame. All that was done by people who believed in their right to dominate.

The notion of endless opportunity for all in the American Dream is routinely invoked by those who are unconcerned about the inequality in capitalism or ignore the deeply embedded white supremacy that continues to live through institutional and unconscious racism.[9] The notion of endless bounty in the American Dream leads people to believe that because such bounty has always been available it will continue to be available through the magic of technology. In America, the dreamers want to believe that the domination of people to clear the frontier was acceptable, and with the frontier gone, that the ever more intense domination of nature to keep the bounty flowing is acceptable.

Of course the United States is not the only place where greed has combined with fantasies of superiority to produce crimes, nor is it the only place where humans have relentlessly degraded ecosystems. But the United States is the wealthiest and most powerful country in the history of the world, and the country that claims for itself a unique place in history, proclaimed by preachers and presidents as "the city upon a hill"[10] that serves as "the beacon to the world of the way life should be," in the words of a U.S. senator.[11] The American Dream is put forward as a dream for all the world to adopt, but it clearly can't be so. Some of the people of the world have had to be sacrificed for the dream, as has the living world. Dreams based on domination are, by definition, limited.

This reinterpretation helps us consider our options for the future. The American Dream typically is illustrated with stories of heroes who live the dream. But the larger story of the American Dream casts the United States itself as the hero on the global stage. We might ask the uncomfortable question: Is the United States an epic hero or a tragic one? Literature scholars argue over the definition of the terms "epic" and "tragedy," but in common usage an epic celebrates the deeds of a hero who is favored by, and perhaps descended from, the gods. These heroes overcome adversity to do great things in the service of great causes. Epic heroes win.

A tragic hero loses, but typically not because of an external force. The essence of tragedy is what Aristotle called "hamartia," an error in judgment made because of some character flaw, such as hubris. That excessive pride of the protagonist becomes his downfall. Although some traditions talk about the sin of pride, most people agree that taking some pride in ourselves is psychologically healthy. The problems come when we elevate ourselves and lose a sense of the equal value of others.

This distinction is crucial in dealing with the American Dream, which people often understand in the context of their own hard work and sacrifice. People justifiably take pride, for example, in having started a small business and making it possible for their children to get a college education, which is one common articulation of the American Dream. But pride in our work turns to hubris when we believe we are special for having worked, as if our work is somehow more ennobling than that of others, as if we worked on a level playing field.

When we fall into hubris individually, the consequences can be disastrous for us and those around us. When we fall into that hubris as a nation—when we ignore the domination on which our dreams are based—the consequences are more dramatic. And when that nation is the wealthiest and most powerful in the world, at a time in history when the high-energy/high-technology society is unraveling the fabric of the living world, the consequences are life-threatening globally.

But here's the good news: While tragic heroes meet an unhappy fate, a community can learn from the protagonist's fall. Even tragic heroes can, at the end, celebrate the dignity of the human spirit in their failure. That may be the task of Americans, to recognize that we can't reverse course in time to prevent our ultimate failure, but that in the time remaining we can recognize our hamartia, name our hubris, and do what we can to undo the damage and offer a different model to those who come after us. That requires not just rethinking U.S. history, but thinking in new ways about human history.

Ecological: Revolutionary consequences

Ask an audience to name the three most important revolutions in human history, and the most common answers are the American, French, and Russian. To understand our current situation, the better answer is the agricultural, industrial, and delusional revolutions. While those national revolutions had dramatic effects, not only on those countries but on the course of the past two centuries, these other revolutions reshaped the lives of every human. As a result of these revolutions, it is unclear how much longer human history will continue. The agricultural, industrial, and delusional revolutions were—to use a current clichéd sports metaphor—real game-changers.

The agricultural revolution started about 10,000 years ago when a gathering-hunting species discovered how to cultivate plants for food and domesticate animals. Two crucial things resulted, one ecological and one political. Ecologically, the invention of agriculture kicked off an intensive human assault on natural systems. While gathering-hunting humans were capable of damaging a local ecosystem in limited ways, the large-scale destruction we cope with today has its origins in agriculture, in the way humans have exhausted the energy-rich carbon of the soil. Human agricultural practices vary from place to place but have never been sustainable over the long term. There are better and worse farming practices, but soil erosion has been a consistent feature of agriculture, which makes it the first step in the entrenchment of an unsustainable human economy based on extraction.[12]

We are trained to think that advances in technology constitute progress, but the "advances" in oil-based industrial agriculture have accelerated the ecological destruction. Soil from large monoculture fields drenched in petrochemicals not only continues to erode but also threatens groundwater supplies and creates dead zones in bodies of water such as the Gulf of Mexico. While it's true that this industrial agriculture has produced tremendous yield increases during the last century, no one has come up with a sustainable system for perpetuating that kind of agricultural productivity. Those high yields mask what Wes Jackson has called "the failure of success": Production remains high while the health of the soil continues to decline dramatically.[13] That kind of "success" guarantees the inevitable collapse of the system. We have less soil that is more degraded, and there are no technological substitutes for healthy soil; we are exhausting and contaminating groundwater; and agriculture is dependent on a fuel source that is running out.

Politically, the ability to stockpile food made possible concentrations of power and resulting hierarchies that were foreign to the band-level gathering-hunting societies that were cooperative in nature. This is not to say that humans were not capable of doing bad things to each other prior to agriculture, but only that large-scale institutionalized oppression has its roots in agriculture. We need not romanticize pre-agricultural life but simply recognize that it was organized in far more egalitarian fashion than what we call "civilization," which was made possible by agriculture.

The industrialization of agriculture was made possible, of course, by the industrial revolution that began in the last half of the eighteenth century in Great Britain, which intensified the magnitude of the human assault on ecosystems and humans' assaults on each other. This revolution unleashed the concentrated energy of coal, oil, and natural gas to run the new steam engines and power the machines in textile manufacturing that dramatically increased productivity. That energy eventually transformed all manufacturing, transportation, and communication, not only creating new ways of making, moving, and communicating, but also radically changing social relations. People were pushed off the land and into cities that grew rapidly, often without planning. World population soared from about 1 billion in 1800 to the current 7 billion.

This move from a sun-powered to a fossil fuel–powered, machine-based world has produced unparalleled material comfort for some. Whatever one thinks of the effect of such levels of comfort on human psychology—in my view, the effect has been mixed[14]—the processes that produce the comfort are destroying the capacity of the ecosystem to sustain human life as we know it into the future, and in the present those comforts are not distributed in a fashion that is consistent with any meaningful conception of justice. In short, our world is unsustainable and unjust; the way we live is in direct conflict with common sense and the ethical principles on which we claim to base our lives. How is that possible? Enter the third revolution.

The delusional revolution is my term for the development of sophisticated propaganda techniques in the twentieth century (especially a highly emotive, image-based advertising-marketing system) that have produced in the bulk of the population (especially in First World societies) a distinctly delusional state of being. Journalism and education, idealized as spaces for rationally based truth-telling, sometimes provide a counter to those propaganda systems, but just as often are co-opted by the powerful forces behind them.

Perhaps the most stunning example of this is that during

the 2000s, as the evidence for human-caused climate disruption became more compelling, the percentage of the population that rejects or ignores that science has increased.[15] Why would people who, in most every other aspect of life accept without question the results of peer-reviewed science, dispute the overwhelming consensus of climate scientists in this case? Some have theological reasons, and for others perhaps it is simply easier to disbelieve than to face the implications. But it's clear that the well-funded media campaigns to create doubt have been effective.[16]

Even those who try to resist the delusions often can't help but be drawn into parts of them; it's difficult to keep track of, let alone understand, all of the fronts on which we are facing serious challenges to a just and sustainable future. As a culture, we collectively end up acting as if unsustainable systems can be sustained because we want them to be. Much of the culture's storytelling—particularly through the dominant storytelling institutions, the mass media—remains committed to maintaining this delusional state. In such a culture, it becomes hard to extract oneself from that story. Singer-songwriter Greg Brown captures the trajectory of this delusional revolution when he speculates that one day, "There'll be one corporation selling one little box/ it'll do what you want and tell you what you want and cost whatever you got."[17]

In summary: The agricultural revolution set us on a road to destruction. The industrial revolution ramped up our speed. The delusional revolution has prevented us from coming to terms with the reality of where we are and where we are heading. That's the bad news. The worse news is that there's still overwhelming resistance in the dominant culture to acknowledging that these kinds of discussions are necessary.

The courage to be realistic, radically

We live in an *industrial* world with a globalized *capitalist* economy organized politically around *nation-states*. Finding a willing audience for even a mild critique of any one of these foundational systems is not easy; suggesting that all three systems should be rethought in fundamental ways seems crazy. Even those who may share similar concerns will say that such radical ideas aren't realistic.

Such critiques are radical, in the foundational sense of the term: going to the root, trying to understand the nature of things. Radical analyses go below the surface to look at the underlying systems and structures of power. In contemporary political discourse, labeling an idea "radical" is an easy way to push it out of view. But the question isn't whether a claim is radical, but whether it makes sense. A call for radical change in systems that are working just fine—systems that were producing a just and sustainable world—would be crazy. Why discard something that works, although perhaps imperfectly? But if it's in the nature of these systems to undermine justice and sustainability, then how realistic is it to accept the systems?

Recognizing the need for radical change doesn't mean we should accept any particular radical analysis or proposal, but rather that we can't discard the analysis or ignore the proposal just because it's radical. At various points in history, critiques of feudalism and serfdom, or white supremacy and slavery, were deemed radical—and they were. Is there any reason to believe it is "realistic" to accept the idea that the systems in which we live are the only systems possible or acceptable, just because some people like them and wish them to continue?

If all this seems unbearably heavy, that's because it is too much to bear. Part of the trick is to take this work seriously, without taking ourselves too seriously. Cultivating a sense of humor is as important as our critical-thinking skills. Singer-songwriter John Gorka captured this when he suggested to me, "We should treat each other as infinitely complex, with all of us capable of very thoughtful ways of being wrong."

When we dare to be radical, life doesn't magically get easier. To take seriously these critical questions about the viability of the nation-state and capitalism in a high-energy, mass-consumption society—to ponder the fate of what James Howard Kunstler calls "a living arrangement with no future"[18]—will not resolve the anxiety discussed in the introduction. But it's possible to replace the anxiety with anguish.

CONCLUSION

The Age of Anguish

Anxiety is typically the result of being placed in situations that we cannot understand or control. We are most anxious when we cannot find a way to make sense of what's happening, and when we feel as if there is nothing we can do to change our circumstances. The first step in overcoming anxiety, then, is understanding, and this book has offered an approach to the critical thinking necessary to deepen that understanding.

When we undertake that task honestly, we will have to face some daunting challenges that likely cannot be met without radical changes in the social, economic, and political systems that define our lives. Even if we were to make such changes, there is no guarantee that we can repair the ecological damage we've already done. Platitudes such as "necessity is the mother of invention" express a hollow technological fundamentalism; simply asserting that we want to solve the problems we have created does not guarantee that we can.

Critical thinking can help us understand, but it doesn't guarantee control. Rigorous intellectual work doesn't magically get us off the runaway train or give us magical powers to stop that train. Traces of that anxiety linger, but I believe that when we think critically and face these challenges, we can transform most of that anxiety into anguish.

Is that the best we can do, trade our anxiety for anguish? Yes. I do think our best hope comes if we can shift from an "Age of Anxiety" to an "Age of Anguish."

Crucial in this shift is understanding anguish not as unhappiness with our personal conditions but rather as a deeper grief over our collective state of being that comes from looking honestly at the state of the world. Most of us would prefer to be happy rather than unhappy, but we also recognize that the frenetic search for happiness does not produce a life well lived or a life worth living. As Wendell Berry has put it so eloquently, we live on "the human estate of grief and joy,"[1] a condition we would be wise to accept. But we live in a consumer culture that is eager to sell us things to divert or derail any unpleasant emotions—that's the basic marketing strategy for everything from fashion to alcohol, to offer us ways to distract or numb ourselves. Shop until you drop, and drink until you pass out. Yet we all know that a meaningful human life is defined by that full range of emotions; we cannot feel the highs of life without being willing to experience the lows.

I feel this anguish—this deep grief not for my own condition in the world but for the condition of the world—not solely because of the problems we face; humans have faced crises in the past. My anguish deepens when I recognize the tenacity of the larger systems out of which the problems arise and the ability of those systems to either co-opt or destroy challenges.

What is the effect of these systems? Our world is increasingly fragile in terms of the political (the absence of meaningful democracy in large-scale political units such as the modern nation-state), economic (the inequalities that exist internal to all capitalist systems and between countries in a world dominated by that predatory capitalism), and ecological (the unsustainable nature of our systems and the lifestyles that arise from them).

Beyond that, I am most disturbed by a cultural and spiritual crisis, a condition that goes to the core of how we understand what it means to be human. Many aspects of the modern mass-mediated, mass-marketed, mass-medicated world can easily strip us of our humanity in ways that slowly leave us incapable of responding to these crises. Along with fretting about the other crises, I worry about that.

When I weigh all these concerns and considerations, I can't help but wonder whether our species is an evolutionary dead-end. Is the same big brain that has allowed us to dominate the entire planet going to be our undoing? There's no way to know, of course, and even if that is the case, it doesn't mean we should give up. No matter how much time we humans have left on the planet, we can do what is possible to make that time meaningful.

This leaves me wanting to conclude by celebrating human beings, which may sound odd, given the rather grim nature of our predicament. But we also should go easy on ourselves, precisely because we are a species out of context, facing a unique challenge—we are the first species that will have to self-consciously impose limits on ourselves if we are to survive. This is no small task, and we are bound to fail often. I believe that our failures will be easier to accept and overcome if we recognize these facts:

- We are animals. For all our considerable rational capacities, we are driven by forces that cannot be fully understood rationally and cannot be completely controlled. We should work to sharpen our critical thinking, but remember not to narrow the scope of that thinking.

- We are band/tribal animals. Whatever kind of political unit we live in, our evolutionary history in band-level societies suggests that we stay as close as possible to relatively small groups, even as we work in larger organizations and political units.
- We are band/tribal animals living in a global world. The consequences of the past 10,000 years of human history have left us dealing with human problems on a global scale, from which we can't retreat. Even if our future is going to demand that we "live locally" to a greater degree, at the moment we have a moral obligation to deal with injustice and unsustainability on a global level. That's especially true for those of us living in affluent societies that over the past 500 years have extracted considerable wealth from others around the world.

What does this mean in practice? I think we should proceed along two basic tracks. First, we should commit some of our energy to the familiar movements that focus on the question of justice and sustainability in this world, especially those of us with privileges that are rooted in that injustice. But I also think there is important work to be done in experiments to prepare for what will come in this new future we can't yet describe in detail. Whatever the limits of our predictive capacity, we can be pretty sure we will need ways of organizing ourselves to help us live in a world with less energy and fewer material goods. We have to all develop the skills needed for that world (such as gardening with fewer chemicals, food preparation and storage, foraging, and basic tinkering), and we will need to recover a deep sense of community that has disappeared from the lives of many of us. This means abandoning a sense of ourselves as consumption machines, which the contemporary culture promotes, and deepening our notion of what it means to be humans in search of meaning. We have to learn to tell different stories about our sense of self, our connection to others, and our place in nature. The stories we tell will matter, as will the skills we learn.

McKibben puts this in terms of a new scale for our work:

> The project we're now undertaking—maintenance, graceful decline, hunkering down, holding on against the storm—requires a different scale. Instead of continents and vast nations, we need to think about states, about towns, about neighborhoods, about blocks. . . . We need to scale back, to go to ground. We need to take what wealth we have left and figure out how we're going to use it, not to spin the wheel one more time but to slow the wheel down. We need to choose safety instead of risk, and we need to do it quickly, even at the sacrifice of growth. We need, as it were, to trade in the big house for something that suits our circumstances on this new Eaarth. We need to feel our vulnerability.[2]

Different people will make choices depending on talents and temperaments; we should all follow our hearts and minds to apply ourselves where it makes sense, given who we are and where we live. After starting with a warning about arrogance, I'm not about to suggest I know best what work people should do. But I will suggest that whatever that work is, it should be done out of anguish. Anguish is not something to run from, but something to embrace. When we are stuck in anxiety we find it hard to act, to do what is needed to move forward. Embracing the anguish of our age allows us to make clear choices about the path on which we want to move forward, even if the destination is unknown and the journey uncertain.

In addition to chronicling the anxiety of his age, W.H. Auden's poem also hinted at this embrace of uncertainty:

> For the new locus is never
> Hidden inside the old one
> Where Reason would rout it out,
> Nor guarded by dragons in distant
> Mountains where Imagination
> Could explore it; the place of birth
> Is too obvious and near to notice,
> Some dull dogpatch a stone's throw
> Outside the walls, reserved
> For the eyes of faith to find.[3]

I don't read Auden to be claiming that Reason and Imagination are of no value as we search for the new locus, but only that they are inadequate by themselves. We must use those skills we have learned but also go beyond, to see with the eyes of faith, which I read to be beyond any particular religious faith.

This is the same spirit I hear when Wes Jackson suggests

118

that we are at a moment in history when it's crucial to ask questions that go beyond the available answers and force our knowledge out of its categories.[4] That doesn't mean abandoning all that has come before, but rather being open to new approaches across traditional disciplines. In this project, we should recognize the importance of specialists and experts, but not surrender to those experts our obligation to make our own judgments. This opening up of our intellectual life is a call to broader participation, with each of us contributing where we can. Each of us can take seriously the goal that writer-activist Scott Nearing set for himself: the quest "to learn the truth, to teach the truth, and to help build the truth into the life of the community."[5]

That process can start with all of us spending time thinking about the kind of world in which we would like to live. This question provides a place to start:

> Which practices, systems, and fundamental conceptions of what it means to be human, are consistent with a sustainable human presence on the earth, respectful of other life, in societies that provide the necessary resources for all people to live a decent life, within a culture that fosters individual flourishing alongside a meaningful sense of collective identity, helping us to take seriously our obligations to ourselves, to each other, and to the non-human world?

We can accept the world into which we are born, or we can accept the challenge to remake the world. Such a project requires all of us, and all that each of us has—our passion and our critical thinking, each tempered by humility. It is at the same time a personal challenge (because each of us has to decide what we are willing to risk in the search for greater understanding) that must be a collective effort (because on our own we are guaranteed to fail).

How can we open an honest conversation about that future? It isn't easy, but it starts with telling the truth, from our own experience. When I put out a call asking people for their own experiences with confronting the anguish, I got many inspiring responses, including one from a 70-year-old woman who lives in a rural intentional community:

> I've lived long enough now to be very aware of how different the world has become, how the cycles of nature are off kilter, how the seasons and the climate have shifted. My garden tells me that food doesn't grow in quite the same patterns, and we either get weeks of rain or weeks of heat and drought. This is the second year in a row that our apple trees do not have apples on them. But most people get their food in grocery stores where the apples still appear, and food still arrives, in season and out, from all over the world. This will soon end, and people won't understand why. They don't see the trouble in the land as I and my friends do. I grieve daily as I look on this altered world. My grandchildren are young adults who think their lives will continue as they have been. Who will tell them? They can't hear me. They, and many others, will have to see the changes for themselves, as I have. I can't imagine that anything else will convince them. My grief for

the world, and for them, is compounded by this feeling of helplessness because there is no way we can have the collective action you speak of when the "collective" is still in denial.

The work of breaking out of denial is less about specific actions and more about the habits and virtues we must cultivate. Far from that rural farm, a 35-year-old woman working in an office in Chicago summed that up:

We really need to take it back to the basics and keep it simple. This reminds me of one of my own quotes I thought of a few months ago—"Be humble or be humiliated." I think I'm a simple person. I try to avoid making things more complex than they have to be. I try to focus more on what I need vs. what I want. "Be humble or be humiliated" is my own personal reminder.

Those responses reflect years of critical thinking, of people employing Reason and Imagination, seeking to see with the eyes of faith, digging in for the long haul. If we are to make a decent future for ourselves and our descendants, we have a lot of hard work to do. One thing I am relatively sure about is that that future won't look like any that this culture has typically imagined. For those of us who have lived in the post–World War II United States, our systems have always assumed endless expansion. Each generation believed it would leave to the next a world with more of everything. But to borrow from John Gorka: "The old future's gone."[6]

The world as we imagined it during the days of unlimited

growth is not the world in which we live or ever will live. After decades of expansion, we will make our way in a world defined by contraction. As Gorka sings: "The old future's dead and gone/ Never to return/ There's a new way through the hills ahead/ This one we'll have to earn."

We should not be afraid to face the death of the old future, nor should we be afraid to try to earn a new one. It is the work of people of conscience throughout the ages, and it is our work today, more than ever. It is the work that allows one to live, joyously, in an Age of Anguish.

Endnotes

Introduction

1. W.H. Auden, *The Age of Anxiety: A Baroque Eclogue*, Alan Jacobs, ed. (Princeton, NJ: Princeton University Press, 1947/2011), pp. 104–105.

2. Andrea Tone, a historian of medicine, has chronicled the history of the drugs prescribed for these disorders in *The Age of Anxiety: A History of America's Turbulent Affair with Tranquilizers* (New York: Basic, 2009).

3. I borrow that phrase and the following framework from Wes Jackson, co-founder and president of the Land Institute. See "The Ecosystem as a Conceptual Tool for Agriculture and Culture," *The Land Report*, June 1996. www.landinstitute.org/vnews/display.v?TARGET=printable&article_id=3aa3e2fe9

4. For an accessible summary of the theories about the development of egalitarian social structures, see Peter Gray, "How Hunter-Gatherers Maintained Their Egalitarian Ways: Three Complementary Theories," *Psychology Today*, May 16, 2011. www.psychologytoday.com/blog/freedom-learn/201105/how-hunter-gatherers-maintained-their-egalitarian-ways-three-complementary

5. Robin Dunbar, *The Human Story* (London: Faber and Faber, 2004). For a video summary, see Robin I.M. Dunbar, "Mind the Gap: Why Humans Aren't Just Great Apes," presentation to Gustavus Adolphus College Nobel Conference XLIV, October 7–8, 2008, St. Peter, Minnesota. http://gustavus.edu/events/nobelconference/2008/dunbar-lecture.php

6. Henry Kendall, a Nobel Prize physicist and former chair of the Union of Concerned Scientists' board of directors, was the primary author of the "World Scientists' Warning to Humanity." www.ucsusa.org/ucs/about/1992-world-scientists-warning-to-humanity.html

7. Bill McKibben, *Eaarth: Making Life on a Tough New Planet* (New York: Times Books/Henry Holt, 2010), p. 2.

8. *Ibid.*, p. 25.

9. www.wholeearth.com/issue/1010/article/196/the.purpose.of.the.whole.earth.catalog

10. Stewart Brand, *Whole Earth Discipline: An Ecopragmatist Manifesto* (New York: Viking Adult, 2009), p. 1.

11. Wes Jackson, "Toward an Ignorance-Based Worldview," *The Land Report*, Spring 2005, pp. 14–16. www.landinstitute.org/vnews/display.v/ ART/2004/10/03/42c0db19e37f4. See also Bill Vitek and Wes Jackson, eds., *The Virtues of Ignorance: Complexity, Sustainability, and the Limits of Knowledge* (Lexington: University Press of Kentucky, 2008).

12. For a useful way of organizing our understanding of our ignorance, see the "Ignorance Map." www.ignorance.medicine.arizona.edu/ignorance. html

Chapter 2

1. One good example is Andrea A. Lunsford, John J. Ruszkiewicz, and Keith Walters, *Everything's an Argument with Readings*, 6th ed. (New York: Bedford/St. Martin's, 2013).

2. See Karin Wilkins, *Questioning Numbers: How to Read and Critique Research* (New York: Oxford University Press, 2010).

3. "Crosseyed and Painless" from the album *Remain in Light*, Sire Records, 1980.

4. An important contribution to our understanding of the complexity of scientific inquiry, and intellectual work more generally, is Thomas Kuhn, *The Structure of Scientific Revolutions*, 3rd ed. (Chicago: University of Chicago Press, 1996).

5. Naomi Klein, "Capitalism vs. the Climate," *The Nation*, November 28, 2011. www.thenation.com/article/164497/capitalism-vs-climate/

6. Karl Popper, *The Logic of Scientific Discovery* (London: Routledge, 2002), pp. 37–38. First published as *Logik der Forschung*, 1935.

Chapter 3

1. Hearing of U.S. House of Representatives Committee for Oversight and Government Reform, October 23, 2008. For a news story on the hearing, see PBS Newshour, "Greenspan Admits 'Flaw' to Congress, Predicts More Economic Problems." www.pbs.org/newshour/bb/business/july-dec08/crisishearing_10-23.html. Video of the exchange is online at www.youtube.com/watch?v=R5lZPWNFizQ.

2. For an analysis of these business efforts, see Alex Carey, *Taking the Risk out of Democracy* (Urbana: University of Illinois Press, 1997).

3. William Sloane Coffin Jr., *Credo* (Louisville, KY: Westminster John Knox Press, 2004), p. 5.

Chapter 4

1. *Citizens United v. Federal Election Commission*, 558 U.S. 50 (2010).

2. Naomi Oreskes and Erik M. Conway, *Merchants of Doubt: How a Handful of Scientists Obscured the Truth on Issues from Tobacco Smoke to Global Warming* (New York: Bloomsbury Press, 2010), pp. 261–262; and Robert Jensen, "The plow and the iPhone: Conservative fantasies about the miracles of the market," Al Jazeera English, January 26, 2012. www.aljazeera.com/indepth/opinion/2012/01/2012124114456348914. html

3. Joseph Stiglitz, *The Price of Inequality: How Today's Divided Society Endangers Our Future* (New York: W.W. Norton, 2012), excerpted on Alternet.org. www.alternet.org/books/155738/joseph_stiglitz%3A_the_price_of_inequality/.

4. G. William Domhoff, "Wealth, Income, and Power, September 2005 (updated July 2011). http://sociology.ucsc.edu/whorulesamerica/power/wealth.html. For helpful data and charts on wealth inequality, see Economic Policy Institute, "State of Working America." www.stateofworkingamerica.org/charts/subject/14.

5. Timothy Noah examines inequality data in 2010 in ten essays in Slate Magazine, "The United States of Inequality." www.slate.com/articles/news_and_politics/the_great_divergence/features/2010/the_united_states_of_inequality/introducing_the_great_divergence.html See also his book *The Great Divergence: America's Growing Inequality Crisis and What We Can Do about It* (New York: Bloomsbury, 2012).

6. For an extensive critique of patriotism, see Chapter 3 of Robert Jensen, *Citizens of the Empire: The Struggle to Claim Our Humanity* (San Francisco: City Lights Books, 2004).

7. INCITE! Women of Color Against Violence, eds., *The Revolution Will Not Be Funded: Beyond the Non-Profit Industrial Complex* (Boston: South End Press, 2009).

Chapter 5

1. I elaborate on my view of God-as-mystery in Robert Jensen, *All My Bones Shake: Seeking a Progressive Path to the Prophetic Voice* (Brooklyn, NY: Soft Skull Press, 2009), pp. 47-49.

2. Mary Daly, *Beyond God the Father: Toward a Philosophy of Women's Liberation* (Boston: Beacon, 1973), p. 19.

Chapter 6

1. Lymari Morales, "Majority in U.S. Continues to Distrust the Media, Perceive Bias," *Gallup Politics*, September 22, 2011. www.gallup.com/poll/149624/majority-continue-distrust-media-perceive-bias.aspx. Also see Pew Research Center for the People and the Press, "Press Accuracy Rating Hits Two Decade Low," September 13, 2009. http://people-press.org/2009/09/13/press-accuracy-rating-hits-two-decade-low/.

2. For an account of the development of objectivity, see David Mindich, *Just the Facts: How "Objectivity" Came to Define American Journalism* (New York: New York University Press, 1998).

3. There is an extensive literature documenting this journalistic practice, beginning with Gaye Tuchman, *Making News: A Study in the Construction of Reality* (New York: Free Press, 1978); Herbert Gans, *Deciding What's News* (New York: Pantheon, 1979); and Mark Fishman, *Manufacturing the News* (Austin: University of Texas Press, 1980).

4. *The Daily Show*, July 12, 2004. www.thedailyshow.com/watch/mon-july-12-2004/wolf-blitzer.

5. For an overview, see Michael Massing, *Now They Tell Us: The American Press and Iraq* (New York: New York Review of Books, 2004).

6. Lawrence Soley, *The News Shapers: The Sources Who Explain the News* (New York: Praeger, 1992).

7. Edward S. Herman and Noam Chomsky, *Manufacturing Consent: The Political Economy of the Mass Media*, rev. ed. (New York: Pantheon, 2002).

8. Garth S. Jowett and Victoria O'Donnell, *Propaganda and Persuasion*, 5th ed. (Thousand Oaks, CA: Sage, 2012), p. 7.

9. Matthew Creamer, "Obama wins! . . . Ad Age's Marketer of the Year," *Advertising Age*, October 17, 2008. http://adage.com/article/moy-2008/obama-wins-ad-age-s-marketer-year/131810/.

10. Elisabeth Bumiller, "Traces of terror: The strategy; Bush aides set strategy to sell policy on Iraq," *New York Times*, September 7, 2002, p. A-1.

Chapter 7

1. The distinction between negative and positive conceptions of liberty originates with Isaiah Berlin, *Four Essays on Liberty* (New York: Oxford University Press, 1970).

2. John Stuart Mill, *On Liberty* (Indianapolis: Hackett, 1859/1978), p. 9.

3. Marilyn A. Friedman, "Individuality without Individualism," *Hypatia*, 3:2 (Summer 1988): 131–137.

4.   George Lakoff and Mark Johnson, *Metaphors We Live By*, 2nd ed. (Chicago: University of Chicago Press, 2003).

5.   Paul H. Thibodeau and Lera Boroditsky, "Metaphors We Think With: The Role of Metaphor in Reasoning," *PLoS One 6*, e16782 (2011). www.plosone.org/article/info%3Adoi%2F10.1371%2Fjournal. pone.0016782

6.   Michelle Alexander, *The New Jim Crow: Mass Incarceration in the Age of Colorblindness* (New York: New Press, 2010).

7.   This metaphor is the basis for Eliza Gilkyson's song "Runaway Train," from the CD *Beautiful World*, Red House Records, 2008.

8.   David Orr, *Down to the Wire: Confronting Climate Collapse* (New York: Oxford University Press, 2009), p. 187.

9.   Quoted in R. C. Lewontin, "In the Beginning Was the Word," *Science*, February 16, 2001, pp. 1263–1264. www.sciencemag.org/content/291/5507/1263.full

10. Lovelock, a Fellow of the Royal Society whose work led to the detection of the widespread presence of CFCs in the atmosphere, warned about humans' attack on Gaia in *The Revenge of Gaia: Earth's Climate Crisis and the Fate of Humanity* (New York: Basic, 2006).

Chapter 8

1.   Hugh Brody, *The Other Side of Eden: Hunter-Gatherers, Farmers and the Shaping of the World* (New York: North Point Press, 2001); Christopher Boehm, *Hierarchy in the Forest: The Evolution of Egalitarian Behavior* (Cambridge, MA: Harvard University Press, 2001).

2.   Richard G. Wilkinson and Kate Pickett, *The Spirit Level: Why Greater Equality Makes Societies Stronger* (New York: Bloomsbury, 2010). For a short video discussing the basic findings, see Richard Wilkinson's TED talk, "How Economic Inequality Harms Societies," July 2011. www.ted. com/talks/richard_wilkinson.html

3.   Robert Jensen and Abe Osheroff, "On the Joys and Risks of Living in the Empire." http://uts.cc.utexas.edu/~rjensen/freelance/abeosheroffinterview.htm; "Abe Osheroff: One Foot in the Grave, the Other Still Dancing," dir. Nadeem Uddin, (Northampton, MA: Media Education Foundation, 2009).

4.   James Truslow Adams, *The Epic of America* (New York: Triangle Books, 1931), p. 404.

5.   *Ibid.*, p. 405.

6.   *Ibid.*, p. 411.

7. *Ibid.*, p. 412.

8. Wes Jackson, *Becoming Native to This Place* (Lexington: University Press of Kentucky, 1994), p. 19.

9. For details, see Robert Jensen, *The Heart of Whiteness: Confronting Race, Racism and White Privilege* (San Francisco: City Lights Books, 2005).

10. This phrase is attributed to Puritan John Winthrop's 1630 sermon, "A Model of Christian Charity," which draws on Jesus's words in the Sermon on the Mount, "You are the light of the world. A city set on a hill cannot be hid" [Matt. 5:14]. The late president Ronald Reagan was fond of describing the United States as a "shining city upon a hill," as he did in his farewell address on January 11, 1989. www.reaganlibrary.com/reagan/speeches/farewell.asp

11. Kay Bailey Hutchison, Senate debate on "Authorization of the Use of United States Armed Forces against Iraq," (S.J. Res. 45) October 9, 2002. http://thomas.loc.gov/cgi-bin/query/Z?r107:S09OC2-0011:

12. David R. Montgomery, *Dirt: The Erosion of Civilizations* (Berkeley: University of California Press, 2007).

13. Wes Jackson, *New Roots for Agriculture* (Lincoln: University of Nebraska Press, 1980), chapter 2.

14. Tim Kasser, *The High Price of Materialism* (Cambridge, MA: MIT Press, 2002).

15. For an example of these poll results, see Gallup, "In U.S., Concerns about Global Warming Stable at Lower Levels," March 14, 2011. www.gallup.com/poll/146606/Concerns-Global-Warming-Stable-Lower-Levels.aspx

16. Frontline, "Climate of Doubt," October 23, 2012. www.pbs.org/wgbh/pages/frontline/climate-of-doubt/

17. Greg Brown, "Where Is Maria?" from the CD *Further In*, Red House Records, 1996.

18. James Howard Kunstler, remarks at the meeting of the Second Vermont Republic, October 28, 2005. www.kunstler.com/spch_Vermont%20Oct%2005.htm

Conclusion

1. Wendell Berry, *The Unsettling of America: Culture and Agriculture*, 3rd ed. (San Francisco: Sierra Club Books, 1996), p. 106.

2. Bill McKibben, *Eaarth: Making Life on a Tough New Planet* (New York: Times Books/Henry Holt, 2010), p. 123.

3. W.H. Auden, *The Age of Anxiety: A Baroque Eclogue*, Alan Jacobs, ed. (Princeton, NJ: Princeton University Press, 1947/2011), p. 106.
4. Wes Jackson, "Toward an Ignorance-Based Worldview," *The Land Report*, Spring 2005, pp. 14–16. www.landinstitute.org/vnews/display.v/ART/2004/10/03/42c0db19e37f4
5. Scott Nearing, *The Making of a Radical: A Political Autobiography* (White River Junction, VT: Chelsea Green Publishing, 2000), p. 56.
6. John Gorka, "Old Future" from the CD *Old Futures Gone*, Red House Records, 2003.

Robert Jensen is a professor in the School of Journalism at the University of Texas at Austin and board member of the Third Coast Activist Resource Center in Austin.

Jensen joined the UT faculty in 1992 after completing his Ph.D. in media ethics and law in the School of Journalism and Mass Communication at the University of Minnesota. Prior to his academic career, he worked as a professional journalist for a decade. At UT, Jensen teaches courses in media law, ethics, and politics.

In addition to teaching and research, Jensen writes for popular media, both alternative and mainstream. His opinion and analytic pieces on such subjects as foreign policy, politics, and race have appeared in papers around the country. He contributes to local organizing in Austin, TX, through his work with the Third Coast Activist Resource Center, http://thirdcoastactivist.org/, and the progressive community center 5604 Manor, http://5604manor.org/.

Robert Jensen can be reached at rjensen@austin.utexas.edu and his articles can be found online at http://uts.cc.utexas.edu/~rjensen/index.html.

ALSO BY ROBERT JENSEN

All My Bones Shake: Seeking a Progressive Path to the Prophetic Voice, (Soft Skull Press, 2009)

Getting Off: Pornography and the End of Masculinity (South End Press, 2007)

The Heart of Whiteness: Confronting Race, Racism and White Privilege (City Lights, 2005)

Citizens of the Empire: The Struggle to Claim Our Humanity (City Lights, 2004)

Writing Dissent: Taking Radical Ideas from the Margins to the Mainstream (Peter Lang, 2002)

CO-AUTHORED, WITH GAIL DINES AND ANN RUSSO

Pornography: The Production and Consumption of Inequality (Routledge, 1998)

CO-EDITED, WITH DAVID S. ALLEN

Freeing the First Amendment: Critical Perspectives on Freedom of Expression (New York University Press, 1995)